A Way Out
of Madness

A WAY OUT OF MADNESS

DEALING WITH YOUR FAMILY AFTER YOU'VE BEEN DIAGNOSED WITH A PSYCHIATRIC DISORDER

Daniel Mackler and Matthew Morrissey

ISPS-US Book Series

authorHOUSE®

AuthorHouse™
1663 Liberty Drive
Bloomington, IN 47403
www.authorhouse.com
Phone: 1-800-839-8640

© 2010 Editorial matters and Part I, Daniel Mackler and Matthew Morrissey; individual chapters from Part II, the contributors

No part of this book may be reproduced, stored in a retrieval system, or transmitted by any means without the written permission of the author.

First published by AuthorHouse 3/11/2010

ISBN: 978-1-4490-8350-2 (e)
ISBN: 978-1-4490-8348-9 (sc)
ISBN: 978-1-4490-8349-6 (hc)

Library of Congress Control Number: 2010901395

Printed in the United States of America
Bloomington, Indiana

This book is printed on acid-free paper.

We dedicate this book to all who have been labeled with serious psychiatric disorders and who seek to live in harmony with themselves—and their families.

Contents

Acknowledgments ix
Editors' Introduction xi

Section I: Learning to Deal with Your Family

1) The Nature of Family Conflict 3
2) The Power of the Family 5
3) When Your Perceptions of Reality Differ from Those of Your Parents 9
4) Understanding Your Role in the Family 13
5) Dealing with Feelings of Shame and Stigma 19
6) Your Relationship with the Mental Health System 25
7) Boundaries: The Basis for Respect 31
8) Dealing with Anger, Frustration, and Grief 39
9) Forgiveness 43
10) Practicing a Healthy Lifestyle 49
11) Dealing With Money 57
12) Getting Help Through Psychotherapy 61
13) Distance Versus Closeness with Your Family 67

Section II: Contributors' Chapters

14) Points of No Return—Turning Points with Family 73
    Annie G. Rogers (with Mary M. Rogers)
15) "If Our David Wants to Try Freedom...": Families as Allies and Allies as Family 81
    David Oaks
16) The Harm of Early Hurt 89
    Carol Hebald
17) The Family Messiah 97
    Matthew Morrissey

18) Attachments Lost And Found 105
    Dorothy W. Dundas
19) Life After Family 113
    Will Hall
20) My Family and I 119
    Joanne Greenberg
21) Patch's Story 125
    Patch Adams
22) Coming Off Psychiatric Drugs, Coming Into Myself 129
    Gianna Kali
23) Best Friends with Mom 135
    Daniel Mackler
24) Listening to Each Other: My Mother and I 143
    Janet Foner
25) What They Don't Tell You, You Can Tell Your Family ... 151
    Oryx Cohen

Index 157

Acknowledgments

We wish to thank the following people for their help, inspiration, and encouragement in bringing this book into the world: Ann-Louise Silver, MD, Robert Whitaker, Lloyd Ross, PhD, Burton Seitler, PhD, Warren Schwartz, PsyD, Ron Unger, LCSW, Dorothy Scotten, PhD, Jim Gottstein, JD, Michael O'Loughlin, PhD, Molly Orner, Al Honig, MD, Orna Ophir, PhD, Dawn Brett, PhD, BCETS, FAAETS, Gail Hornstein, PhD, Ashley McNamara, and Edmond DeGaiffier, LICSW.

You have guided, taught, listened, given valuable feedback—and proofread too! Without you this book would not have come into being.

We also give a special thanks to Brian Koehler, PhD, the president of **ISPS-US** (the United States Chapter of the International Society for the Psychological Treatments of the Schizophrenias and Other Psychoses).

We are grateful to be the first published book in the ISPS-US series.

Editors' Introduction

The purpose of this guidebook is to help people diagnosed with psychiatric disorders learn to deal most effectively with their families—and primarily their parents. The book is divided into two sections. We, the editors, have written the first section, which comprises about half the book. This is the "how-to" section: how to deal with a range of issues that commonly come up in the struggle to improve family relationships and lessen family conflict.

The second section is written by contributors, each of whom tells the personal story of how he or she learned to find a balance with his or her family of origin. Each contributor has "been there"—been psychiatrically diagnosed, primarily with either schizophrenia or bipolar disorder. Additionally, almost all of the contributors, at one point or another, have experienced psychiatric medication, hospitalization, physical restraint, and some even electroshock therapy.

Some of the contributors are well-known. Joanne Greenberg, for instance, wrote the world-famous and bestselling novel *I Never Promised You a Rose Garden*, a slightly fictionalized account of her recovery from schizophrenia. And Patch Adams, the doctor immortalized by actor Robin Williams in the movie *Patch Adams*, tells about his psychiatric hospitalizations and his relationship with his family—and how they ultimately helped him not just to recover but to find his life's path.

Other contributors are less well-known. We have college professors, authors, therapists, psychiatric survivors, psychiatric advocates, community leaders, a well-respected internet blogger—even an ex-Broadway actress.

For all their differences, most of the contributors share three main facets. First, none is presently diagnosed with a psychiatric disorder. Second, none is presently a "consumer" in the psychiatric system. And third, almost none takes psychiatric medication any longer. All have essentially recovered, and have a correspondingly similar perspective on their psychiatric history—and their relationships with their families—that we found so valuable, even inspirational.

Our book holds to the vision of full recovery. We do so not

just because we find this vision hopeful, but because it is a realistic possibility for many people. Although many textbooks (and conventional wisdom) suggest that recovery, especially recovery without psychiatric medication, is rare or even impossible, there are highly respected scientific studies within the psychiatric literature,[1] including an important World Health Organization study,[2] that show the commonality of full recovery. Sadly, the great majority of mental health professionals today, not to mention the media and the general public, are unaware of this. Over and over again we hear the familiar message: "You have a biologically-based brain disease and you'll need medications for the rest of your life." Although we acknowledge that psychiatric drugs can and do help some people, we find the message that they are universally necessary for serious psychiatric disorders to be one that robs many of hope, strips them of dignity, and denies them the inborn resiliency that makes us human.

Still, we also want to avoid a kind of naïveté that spreads false hope. We, the two main writers, are both practicing outpatient psychotherapists who work with people diagnosed with severe psychiatric disorders, and we realize how difficult full recovery can be for some. Although we have both seen people who have recovered fully, we have also seen people who recover in other ways. We recognize that recovery exists on a spectrum, and we have great respect for all people, regardless of their degree of recovery. Some people take medication for years and may wish to continue it for the rest of their lives. We respect their choice. Others wish to end their medication, and we respect this choice too, though we cannot state strongly enough the danger in stopping medication abruptly, much less without medical advice and social support.[3]

Similarly, the range of ways that people resolve family conflict

---

[1] C. Harding, "The Vermont Longitudinal Study of Persons with Severe Mental Illness," *American Journal of Psychiatry* 144 (1987): 727-734; M. Harrow and T. Jobe, "Factors involved in outcome and recovery in schizophrenia patients not on antipsychotic medications: a 15-year multifollow-up study." *The Journal of Nervous and Mental Disease*, May, 2007, 195(5): 406-14. See also various studies presented in Robert Whitaker's classic exposé of psychiatry, *Mad in America*: R. Whitaker (2002). *Mad in America: Bad Science, Bad Medicine, and the Enduring Mistreatment of the Mentally Ill*. Cambridge, MA: Perseus Publishing.

[2] A. Jablensky (1992). *Psychological Medicine*. Supplement 20, pages 1-95.

[3] For more on the dangers of stopping medication abruptly, see: P. Breggin (1991). Toxic Psychiatry. New York: St. Martin's Press.

is as broad as the range of humanity. Some people continue to live in their parents' homes as they struggle toward balance, while others go in an opposite direction and find their balance by taking significant distance from their families, both geographically and emotionally. Other people try a middle path or a combination of different paths.

Our philosophy is this: Your path is yours to discover.

For that reason, as you read this book we encourage you to "take what you like and leave the rest." We are here to provide ideas and options. Although some of what we share here might apply to you, some might not. You know yourself better than any "expert" knows you, and what life has taught us is that the truth is within you—as is the whole template for your recovery.

Our best hope is that this book will guide you to look within, and if you can do that, then our mission will have succeeded.

Section I

Learning to Deal with Your Family

Chapter 1

The Nature of Family Conflict

Families can be wonderful—and also difficult. Some degree of conflict with your family, and particularly your parents, is a normal and expected part of development into independent adulthood. Yet when you experience severe emotional problems, particularly those that get diagnosed as mental disorders or lead to psychiatric hospitalizations, these conflicts are often heightened. This can disrupt your process of developing into the unique person you were meant to become. This disruption, if not resolved properly, can so easily leave you stuck and frustrated in your life.

This can throw your entire family into further turmoil, worsening your dilemma. Frustrations that were previously buried can rise to the surface, and old wounds, dormant sometimes for decades, can erupt. This can be an extremely painful time, both for you and your family. This is a time when the most support is needed—and yet a time when it is most difficult for family members to support one another.

Regrettably, people diagnosed with psychiatric disorders often find few available resources to guide them. Although good therapy and good peer support can be immensely helpful, they are not always available—and in many cases are rare.[4] It is all too common that well-meaning peers and professionals simply cannot relate to what goes on behind the closed doors of your family home—and in your mind. They have never experienced it, perhaps have never

---

[4] That said, at the present time, more than perhaps any other in history, the psychiatric peer support movement is growing in leaps and bounds—internationally. Groups like the National Empowerment Center, the Freedom Center (founded by Will Hall and Oryx Cohen, who both wrote chapters in this book), The Icarus Project, MindFreedom International (founded by David Oaks, who also wrote a chapter in this book), and the international Hearing Voices Network, to name but a few, prove incredibly useful and supportive to many—and have all been founded for and by psychiatric survivors.

even considered it, which makes it difficult for them to translate their experience into something useful and healing for you.

The same is often true with your parents and family. Although they may love you, and have a desperate urge to help you, this love may not be the love you need—and may actually hinder your forward progress, despite their best intentions. They may think they understand what is going on in your life and in your thoughts, but that does not always mean they do. Sometimes your inner world is just too painful for them to comprehend, especially if they feel partially responsible. This, however, may not stop them from *thinking* they know what is best for you. This can leave you feeling controlled, judged, and even stigmatized, which at the very least can be frustrating, and at the worst disempowering and alienating. This not only impedes your recovery but can also heighten the intensity of family conflict.

We aim to provide you with a measure of understanding and support—and new ideas. We wish to share the best of our experience on what it takes to achieve a life of increased balance with your family, and ultimately a wider life of inner tranquility. We have seen firsthand just how family conflict can wreak havoc on recovery, and by the same token we have witnessed again and again how family support—strong, loving, respectful family support—can, if you can develop it, be a wonderfully healing asset. Although we recognize that not every family situation will ultimately develop into an optimally supportive situation, we strongly believe that the resolution of serious family conflict *is* possible for everyone, and that you, through your increased understanding and actions, can steer your life in this direction.

Questions for Self-Reflection

1) What is the nature of my conflict with my family?
2) How long has this conflict been going on?
3) How does my family conflict affect me?
4) What kind of a relationship would I prefer with my family members?
5) Can I acknowledge that there is some hope for me to improve my relationship with my family members?

Chapter 2

The Power of the Family

The family is one of the most powerful forces in the universe, on par with gravity, electricity, and momentum. The simplest way to observe this is to see how quickly we change when we spend concentrated time around our families after being away for a period. How easily we slip into old patterns we thought we had long since given up. This change can sometimes be quite pronounced in people diagnosed with mental disorders. Many find they can be quite well-adjusted and even tranquil and self-loving when they are away from their families, only to find their tranquility disrupted when they step back into their families. Some people even return to hearing voices or having delusional thoughts as a consequence.[5] At other times, the change is milder, with people feeling depressed, confused, withdrawn, or self-doubting after being around their families. Holidays—a time of historical closeness with the family—can be particularly intense, with flare-ups of all varieties of emotional conflict, even with people who have great love and respect for their families.

Other people, however, feel lost, isolated, and even hopeless when they are *away* from their families. They feel a sense of massive relief when they return. Their families constitute a domain of comfort and nurturance, one not always easy to recreate in the outer world, especially if one feels different or alienated from peers.

Family, be it positive or negative, is a charged equation for everyone. No one is neutral about his or her family. And this should be no surprise. Our personalities were formed within the heat, pressure, and intimacy of our families. Our families were our first contact with other human beings, and provided us our original templates for how to relate to one another. They provided our primary role model for acceptable behavior. Early on we internalized as normal their combination of love and un-love, and

---

[5] See Will Hall's chapter (Chapter 19) for more on this.

our personalities—both our strengths and our weaknesses—adjusted in relation to this. In time, as we grew, we came to witness alternate ways of relating to others, which gave us perspective on our families and helped us realize the relative strengths and weaknesses of our origins. But that did not always change the imprinted make-up of who we were and who we are.

Some people feel that their families are responsible for having created their mental or emotional problems. Although the degree to which this may or may not be true is beyond the scope of this book, one thing is clear: families can have a profound effect on the course of a person's emotional life and, specifically, the course of a psychiatric disorder. People whose families are deeply supportive in mature and healthy ways tend to do far better than those whose families are unsupportive, judgmental, stigmatizing, or even over-involved.

It is our hope that through the course of this book you maximize the benefit you derive from your family. This may be no small feat. Although your family may wield incredible power over you, and seem to control the reins of your life—perhaps guiding your psychiatric treatment, dispensing your money, hospitalizing you if they decide, choosing your therapist (and even your medications), evicting you from your bedroom, perhaps even setting your adult curfew—you retain a massive amount of power to change things for the better. Contrastingly, if you do not handle your potential power optimally, you might also change things for the worse.

This book encourages you to seek within yourself your own center of healthy power and to nourish it. This, along with many of the points we make in this book, is easier said than done. Old habits die hard, and sometimes not only we, but our parents and families, resist change. Like us, they may be quite locked into ancient patterns and ancient relationships. Many parents find it difficult to watch their now-adult child grow up, and sometimes, despite the best intentions and with no conscious desire, might contribute to keeping him or her stuck.[6]

This makes your task, the task of taking back your power and striving toward independence—mental independence first and foremost—all the more challenging. But it is by no means impossible.

---

[6] For more on this see: A. Napier and C. Whitaker (1988). *The Family Crucible.* New York: Harper.

And it is this that sets the stage for a much more fulfilling, and empowered, life.

Questions for Self-Reflection

1) In what ways does my family have power over me? In what ways do they not have power over me?
2) In what ways are my family members important to me in my life?
3) In what ways do I slip into old patterns when I spend time with my family members?
4) Do I like or respect my own behavior when I'm around my family?
5) In what ways am I different when I am not around my family?
6) In what ways do my family members encourage and impede my path toward independence?

Chapter 3

When Your Perceptions of Reality Differ from Those of Your Parents

Each of us has his or her own unique perception of reality. That is part of being human. Although we may enjoy the challenge of interacting with people with alternate points of view, we usually tend to gravitate toward those with whom we share things in common. Many people are uncomfortable around others whose perspectives are radically different from their own. For this reason, some people avoid interacting with people of foreign cultures, avoid speaking in foreign languages, even avoid eating foreign foods. Likewise, many people are uncomfortable with a person diagnosed with a mental disorder, because he or she experiences reality differently.

This does not mean, however, that your perception of reality is necessarily wrong or inaccurate. Any study of the "mad" geniuses throughout history should be enough to dispel that myth.[7] Also, sometimes people are diagnosed with mental disorders *because* their all-too-true perception of reality *is too painful for the norm to accept.* Our world has a long history of pathologizing—and marginalizing, stigmatizing, even medicating—truth-tellers. We, as therapists, have even witnessed people being labeled "delusional" or "paranoid," on top of whatever other disorders with which they might be diagnosed, for resisting *being medicated!*

Families may become uncomfortable when one of their members sees things differently than they do. This is part of the reason

---

[7] Sir Isaac Newton was considered to have been "psychotic" at points (some label him as having been "bipolar"), and yet he was one of the most influential scientific thinkers in the history of mankind. Van Gogh—perhaps the most famous artist of the last two hundred years—was also considered to have been "mad" at points. And John Nash, one of the most brilliant mathematicians of the modern era (and the subject of the film *A Beautiful Mind*), was diagnosed with schizophrenia—and unlike in the film, which distorted his story, he recovered fully without the help of antipsychotic medication.

teenagers clash with their parents. The parent says "I know what is right and best for you," and the teenager does not agree. This family clash can be even more heightened when a person, now an adult, is diagnosed with a psychiatric disorder. Perhaps you hear things that other people cannot hear. Perhaps you see or feel things that others do not consider to exist. Perhaps you understand things or perceive things or think things out in a way that others cannot conceptualize. Perhaps you have fears or beliefs that others do not share. Perhaps you speak in ways or on levels that others cannot understand. And perhaps you tell the truth in a way that frightens them.

Often others will want to squelch, rather than embrace, your differences. Maybe they are not as tolerant as you would like them to be, and it can seem that *you* always have to be the one who adjusts to their perceptions. Perhaps you have learned to keep quiet about what you perceive, because if you express your point of view they only take more distance from you, which makes your life even more alienating and isolating, not to mention painful. It's hard enough to see the world through different eyes than those of everyone else, let alone to be marginalized further if you talk about it, much less argue it. Others would much prefer if you just "quit being so different" and lived life their way. If only it were so easy!

So how do you deal with your family when your perceptions differ from theirs? Shutting yourself down and going silent generally only makes things worse, yet so too can opening up. This is like living between a rock and a hard place, and not surprisingly can produce much anxiety, which clouds your judgment and leads to feelings of desperation and pressure.

Yet it is possible for your family to appreciate—and not pathologize—some of your perceptions. And maybe it is possible for you first to share *not* your perceptions, but your feelings of alienation and isolation *around your perceptions*. For instance, if you thought the room was bugged with microphones and you knew your family would react negatively to this ("oh c'mon, you're *paranoid!*"), instead of talking about microphones you might instead tell them, "I don't exactly feel comfortable sharing my perceptions, but I *will say* that I feel very alone and frightened with my ideas, and that is hard." Many times this works in eliciting empathy from people who are otherwise closed off to giving it.

Likewise, perhaps *you* can be more respectful of *their* alternate perceptions of reality, and *their* feelings of alienation from you. If they could have their magic wish they would probably want you to adopt their point of view, but isn't it true that if you could have *your* wish you would probably have them see things *your* way? Unfortunately this rarely happens. Perhaps instead you and they can both learn to become more tolerant of your mutual differences. Accomplishing this inherently improves family relationships—and your overall life. This takes time, and hard work on your part, but the good news is that it is possible. In subsequent chapters we will address various ways to accomplish it.[8]

Also, there may be things you can learn from them. Maybe some of their ideas, even if they do not express them well or express them in the most loving way, have some relevance for you. Perhaps, as a possible example, they are able to see, in ways that you might miss, the negative impact of isolation on your life. Or perhaps they have ideas for things you might do or try—support groups, for instance—that you have not considered. Here it is vital for you to embrace the message—without getting lost in the style of the messenger. Perhaps your family has hounded you to change your ways for so long and with such intensity that you defend yourself and your perspective by ignoring everything they say. You wouldn't be the first to do this! We all do this to some degree or other, and it forms the basis of whatever rigidity or inflexibility we might have.

Your challenge is to be flexible—and humble. Others might not be, but we cannot control them. We can only control ourselves. Ideally we can strive to look within ourselves, trust our hearts and souls enough to listen deeply to what others have to tell us—and struggle to learn from them. You may not agree with their ideas, and their ideas might in fact be dead wrong, but we can even learn from that. We often learn the most from those who have a radically alternate perspective to ours. This is not easy, though if we can find it within ourselves to trust others, even for a single solitary moment, we do ourselves a great service.

---

[8] See Oryx Cohen's chapter (Chapter 25) for more on this—on how he managed to help his family (and particularly his parents) come to understand his point of view more clearly, and in a way that greatly benefited him.

Questions for Self-Reflection

1) How do my perceptions of reality differ from the perceptions of my family members?
2) In what ways do my family members and I pressure each other to adopt each other's viewpoints?
3) In what ways might I be more accepting of their differing versions of reality? What might I be able to learn from them?
4) In what ways do these points of differing perceptions of reality cause friction in my family?
5) In what ways might I be able to share my feelings of hurt or loneliness with my family without causing a fight or conflict?
6) What, if anything, might I be doing to contribute to family conflict?
7) Are there ways I talk to my family members that prevent better communication?

Chapter 4

Understanding Your Role in the Family

We all grow up playing roles in our families, and more intensely and rigidly so in more troubled families. Family roles and family dynamics are generally unspoken and unconscious, especially in families with a higher degree of conflict. Sometimes these roles can be somewhat healthy and prepare us for a strong, independent adult life. Yet other times they can literally cripple us. Understanding your own historical role or roles in your family offers you the key to make more informed choices about your present life, to modify the way you interact with the world, and ultimately to unfold your life and your future. As the saying goes, "The truth will set you free."

Some family therapists even go so far as to see psychiatric disorders as an expression or a facet of troubled family dynamics.[9] They share the observation that when family dynamics begin to shift for the better—in more loving, respectful, and supportive directions and away from hostility, high emotion, and conflict—the psychiatric disorder of individual family members can become much milder, or even go away entirely. Furthermore, it has been argued by some that it is not even individuals who are "mentally ill," but whole systems—cultures, societies, and, perhaps most potently, families.[10] Sometimes the people who get labeled with a psychiatric disorder are just the token carriers of the larger problem. Everyone else in

---

[9] J. Haley (1973). *Uncommon Therapy: The Psychiatric Techniques of Milton H. Erickson, M.D.* New York and London: W.W. Norton. See also: 1) Alice Miller (1997). *The Drama of the Gifted Child.* New York: Basic Books. 2) J. Haley (1997). *Leaving Home: The Therapy of Disturbed Young People.* New York: Routledge. 3) Boszormenyi-Nagy, I. and Framo, J. (eds.) (1965) *Intensive Family Therapy: Theoretical and Practical Aspects.* New York: Heber Medical Division/Harper & Row.

[10] See: E. Goffman (1959). *The Presentation of Self in Everyday Life.* Garden City, NY: Anchor Books.

the system merely expresses the greater problem latently or in more socially acceptable ways.[11]

So, in that way one might argue that being "mentally ill"—or having patterns of behavior that get labeled "mentally ill"—*is itself a role in the family or culture*. It, like every role, can serve a purpose. Yet how, one might ask, could having behaviors that get labeled as a psychiatric disorder serve the family in any positive way, and why in the world would *anyone* take on such a role? This question seems counterintuitive, as clearly a psychiatric disorder wreaks havoc on the family in so many ways. But does it always?

Sometimes an emotionally troubled child, now grown to adulthood, can serve to maintain family stability. For instance, if one child stays behind and needs extra care and attention, this allows parents to maintain their parental role for many extra years and sometimes decades. Although many parents might be miserable about this, others find a degree of comfort in it: there can be a great satisfaction and feeling of usefulness in being a parent, sometimes even a beleaguered parent. In other cases, a troubled adult child can save a parental marriage that might otherwise have ended in divorce. It is hard to have an "empty nest"—a contributing factor to so many divorces—when your child never leaves home or demands all your attention.

There are also times when a diagnosis of a psychiatric disorder can be related to the myths of the entire family. Most families believe certain myths about themselves that are not quite true but serve to maintain family stability. Sometimes the person diagnosed with the psychiatric disorder can be the strongest defender of these myths, to the point of absurdity—*and a diagnosis*. At other times, the diagnosis can represent the person swinging to the opposite extreme and rejecting those very myths—or adamantly rebelling against them—to the frustration not only of the family but to the society that might be sharing some of these very myths.

But often it is difficult for a family or even a society to look at itself closely enough to understand the role of the person in its midst who is diagnosed with a psychiatric disorder. Isn't it just easier to say that a psychiatric disorder is the result of bad genetics or a chemical imbalance or a faulty shake of life's dice?

We would reply in this way: look at all the people who have

---

[11] See: S. Minuchin (1970). *Family Healing: Strategies for Hope and Understanding.* New York: The Free Press.

recovered fully from a severe psychiatric disorder and gone on to lead highly mature, satisfied, productive lives. Look at how their brain chemicals readjusted, how their genetics failed to impede their healing, and how their faulty shake of life's dice shifted for the better.

Yet it can be extremely difficult to recover—and to change one's way of interacting with and viewing one's family and one's society. This requires massive amounts of growth and independence, and this is almost never easy, whether a person has been diagnosed or not. Often it is simply terrifying to grow up and face new challenges, even with family support (though sometimes a family's way of supporting, by jumping in and trying to help, can prove to be unhelpful). Regardless, the anxiety inherent in this process of struggling for growth and independence can be overwhelming—and itself can lead to breakdown. It is not surprising that most people diagnosed with schizophrenia have what is labeled their "first psychotic break" in their late teens and early twenties—a time of incredible stress and transition, where new roles and expectations abound. Sometimes it is easier to retreat into a private world, a private reality, and a protected family system of familiar expectations, familiar people, familiar myths, and even a familiar setting.

Meanwhile, let us look at some family roles to study what purposes each serve for the family system, and how each has the potential to throw off an individual's emotional balance:

The Nurturer: The Nurturer plays the role of caretaking his or her[12] parents or other family members. Starting in some cases as young as one or two years old, he is sensitive to their feelings and needs, their wounds, their anger, and puts forth his best energy to assuage them. This gives him a sense of purpose and self-esteem. It also maintains the stability of his parents, filling their inner void, giving them the love they either never got as children or do not presently get in sufficient quantities from their spouse or friends. The Nurturer lives with a massive sense of internal pressure to "be there" for others and take inappropriate responsibility for them—at the expense of himself and his own legitimate needs. This can malform the foundation of his sense of self, stunt his development,

---

[12] We apologize for the overuse of the word "he" and "him" (and underuse of "she" and "her") in this book. We do so only for simplicity of language and not to exclude a female perspective.

and leave him with a twisted sense of guilt for wanting to break away. And all of this prevents him from being able to seek and find his own equal companions on life's journey. He lives with a huge void within, and if his role collapses—which can easily happen if something disrupts his relationships with those he caretakes—he risks spiraling into nothingness and even into psychosis.

The Hero: The Hero is the child cultivated for ultimate success in the world. He grows up to become a leader, a torch-bearer, a bastion of strength and maturity. He carries all the family's seemingly positive qualities, and receives self-esteem, praise, and admiration in return. But, as with the role of the Nurturer, being a Hero can create a terrible sense of responsibility within a person, because even the most talented, brilliant, and successful person cannot be perfect all the time. And when this success fails, which may be inevitable on life's stormy path, there's nothing left behind the Hero's façade but the emptiness of breakdown—and sometimes deep psychological breakdown.

The Scapegoat: The Scapegoat is the lightning rod for the family's split-off and repressed anger, rage, and hatred. Every family, especially a traumatized family, holds hidden negativity, and often it cannot be expressed toward the people or situations that really deserve it. So the child playing the role of the Scapegoat becomes its convenient receptacle. He gets humiliated, smacked, tormented, blamed, put down, teased, bullied, even sexually abused.[13] This maintains the family's troubled equilibrium. As he grows up he may even mold his behavior into unhealthy or seemingly "punishable offenses" so that he makes their job of rationalizing their abusiveness all the more easy and convenient. He derives a warped sense of self-esteem from this, because even though his role is overtly self-abusive, he knows he is important to the family system. The problem is, this abuse permeates him, throws off his healthy self-perception, and sets him up for a lifetime of abusive relationships, self-hatred, and stigma. On the other hand, heaven forbid the Scapegoat insists on putting a stop to his family's abusiveness, for then he discovers a deeper truth: that they have little other use for him. He then ends up even more rejected, marginalized, and alienated—or worse—and

---

[13] See Carol Hebald's chapter (Chapter 16). She was a classic Scapegoat in her family of origin.

now finds himself without even a role that serves the family. This can drive anyone over the edge of sanity.

The Broken One: The Broken One is ever in need of family members' help. Although all children need help and love, and in massive quantity, the Broken One becomes a bottomless pit of need, and unconsciously keeps digging the bottom deeper. He cannot seem to take care of himself properly, and always needs others to fight his battles, guide his way, clean up his messes, correct for his errors, and take responsibility for him, long after these needs have become age-inappropriate. Families can derive great self-esteem from caring for him, because they get to feel strong and mature and powerful in comparison to him. Secretly they say, "He's the problem, not us!" He is the perpetual victim, and his family rewards him for it with extra attention, nurturance, and caring. His problem, however, is that all their over-the-top caring and support prevent him from growing strong. He lives his life on the wooden crutches of his family, so when the time comes for him to become independent and leave them he risks falling flat on his face.

We realize that we have listed only a few of the basic roles that people play in their families. There are many other roles, or combinations of roles, that people play. Some of the other roles include, but are not limited to, the Mascot, the Bully, the Addict, and the Enabler. For an excellent book on roles and family dynamics in general, we recommend Virginia Satir's book *The New Peoplemaking*.[14]

So, to recap, your job is to study and understand your role in the family. If you can do this you will derive the strength that only insight can bring. If you do not understand your role, you risk becoming unwittingly vulnerable to the weaknesses inherent in each role, and to play out these roles throughout your adult life. Knowledge is power—and we hope you take it.

---

[14] V. Satir. (1988). *The New Peoplemaking*. Palo Alto, CA: Science and Behavior Books.

Questions for Self-Reflection

1) What was or were my historical role or roles in my family when I was growing up?
2) How did these roles affect my development as a growing person?
3) In what ways did this role(s) shift over time?
4) To what degree am I still playing the same role I was raised to play?
5) What are the roles of my other family members?
6) In what ways do I like versus dislike my role(s) in my family?
7) How would I ideally like to change my role in the family?

Chapter 5

Dealing with Feelings of Shame and Stigma

Shame is a fundamental and basic emotion. It has been found in all cultures and is recognized by telltale signs: blushing, a lowered head, a sense of unpleasant warmth, downcast eyes, a slack posture, and mental confusion. It is a normal response to feelings of humiliation, disgrace, dishonor, and a sense of inadequacy.

The whole process of being diagnosed with a mental disorder, especially if you have been hospitalized, brings on intense feelings of shame. Perhaps you feel as if you've made a mess of your life, that life has defeated you, that you will never make it, even that you let down your friends and family. Perhaps people view you differently, even stigmatize you.

The word "stigma" comes to us from the Ancient Greek word for "tattoo." It was common in the ancient world for soldiers, slaves, and devotees of religious temples to be tattooed. Nowadays, when you get diagnosed with a mental disorder, it is like your mind has been tattooed with a mark of social disgrace. The ink used to tattoo you is made from pure and concentrated shame. You get a branding that is hard to remove. And even if you yourself remove it, others do not necessarily forget so quickly—and can quickly remind you of it.

It is a sad fact that people labeled with mental disorders are looked down upon as "lessers," seen as "crazy," "nuts," "insane," unstable, even inherently violent. This stigmatization can be devastating—and cause a massive erosion of self-esteem. It is hard to turn on the television or read the newspaper without hearing shameful and prejudiced stigmatization of people diagnosed with mental disorders. This makes it almost impossible to feel safe and open in the world. The natural response in this circumstance is to feel only more shame—and to become silent.

And yet the television and newspaper are not the worst places to feel stigmatized. Social situations can be even worse. Shame and stigma are always there, lurking in the background. For example, what do you say in a casual encounter if an acquaintance asks what you've been up to lately? You generally don't say, "Oh, I'm getting over a nervous breakdown, where I got diagnosed with schizophrenia, and I'm piecing my life back together." Instead you give a vague answer that usually puts a stop to the social interaction, because the other person senses that something is amiss. This inwardly leaves you to feel the sting of shame—and perhaps also the terror of getting further questioned by others. Even talking to your closest friends and family about your mental health can be fraught with opportunities for misunderstanding.[15] It is hard to trust people to be nonjudgmental.

Loss of Social Position

Hand-in-hand with the difficulty in social encounters is the devastating loss of social position. Maybe you have been fired from your job, have lost your housing, or have had to leave college to return home. Perhaps you did and said things during your breakdown that you now regret. Perhaps others are no longer so accepting of you—or even avoid you. Perhaps you feel marked as an outcast by society. Again, shame is the inevitable result. So, too, is alienation and marginalization—and loss of self-esteem.

Joanne Greenberg, the bestselling author of *I Never Promised You a Rose Garden* (and author of Chapter 20 of this volume), was hospitalized for three years with a diagnosis of schizophrenia. For years after her recovery from psychosis—a full and ongoing recovery that has lasted more than fifty years—she had to deal with the shame and stigma of her past diagnosis, even though she has not carried that diagnosis since the early 1950s. For instance, even after recovering she had the letters "MP"—for "Mental Patient"—stamped on her driver's license. She also legally had to carry "Sanity Papers" to prove that she really was recovered. She solved this humiliating bind by moving to a different state that had more respectful laws—and didn't require the stamp of "MP" on her license.[16]

---

[15] See Dorothy Dundas's chapter in this book. (Chapter 18.) Although she has recovered from her history of severe mental distress for forty years, she has still spoken hardly one word to her family about her diagnosis or painful history of psychiatric hospitalizations.

[16] Largely unpublished interview by Daniel Mackler with Joanne Greenberg, August, 2007. (Portions of Greenberg's interview appeared in Mackler's 2008 film, *Take These Broken Wings*, on recovery from schizophrenia without psychiatric medication.

Similarly, when she published her bestselling memoir, her family did not want her to use her real name on the cover, because that would bring shame upon their family. The neighbors and relatives might find out![17] So she published *I Never Promised You a Rose Garden* under a pseudonym. It took several years before she actually attached her real name to it.

Many people burdened with shame retreat socially. At times it is easiest to retreat to the hidden nest of their families, which can increase the strain on family relationships. Yet what happens if your family is ashamed of you too, and ashamed of themselves as well because of your history? This can be so painful, and certainly increases the tension in your home. Perhaps your parents had high expectations for you and even projected their own life's unfulfilled hopes and dreams onto you. Now they are dealing with their own letdown because of the things you are going through. And this does not make it any easier for you, because of course you can sense their feelings.

Although this difficult time in your life would be the logical time for them to be most supportive of you, sometimes it works in the opposite direction. Often parents are now the most frustrated, most upset, and most confused, and do not always behave in the most mature and gentle way. Perhaps they are even angry at you and blame you for your problems—as if you chose them. And perhaps secretly they blame themselves and are so full of anger at themselves that they take it out on you. Arguments and accusations become common now, sometimes followed by periods of silence and non-interaction. This certainly does not help you, and can hurt terribly.

All this can lead a person diagnosed with a mental disorder to get stuck in a cycle of shame. Everything you do and see can remind you of your breakdown, which only causes more shame. Nothing seems to help. This leads to an increasing sense of misery and hopelessness, resulting in depression and apathy. The conventional mental health system, and perhaps even your family, can view these as additional symptoms of your mental diagnosis, thus "warranting" more medication, and perhaps even hospitalization. Many people in this situation feel an unspoken conviction, however untrue, that they are permanently broken or defective.

---

[17] Also from largely unpublished interview by Daniel Mackler with Joanne Greenberg, August, 2007.

In other cases, the situation might cause you to become even more defensive, even to the point of absolutely denying that there is any mental or emotional problem at all. All too often this just gives those around you more cause to label your ideas as disturbed, which only tends to add to your feelings of hopelessness.

This hopeless feeling, regardless of its origin, makes it shockingly easy for you to slide into the role of chronic mental patient.

Breaking the Cycle of Shame

So how do you avoid the buildup of chronic shame, or, if you are in its grip, how do you escape?

The key to breaking the shame cycle is to experience real life successes. This takes time, and starts slowly and in small ways, though in some cases it can happen quickly, especially with a shift of environment. We have witnessed cases in which a simple shift from a shameful, stigmatizing environment to a non-shameful, non-stigmatizing environment is enough to help someone emerge significantly from psychosis.[18]

By real life successes we mean experiences like getting back into the workforce or school, developing positive, uplifting relationships, or returning to activities that once brought you joy and excitement. We will address this subject in much more depth in later chapters. For now, though, it is sufficient to say that nothing counteracts feelings of shame more than having a sense of social purpose and life direction. In a sense, this ties in to the previous chapter on your role in the family system. Having a sense of meaningful social purpose is a role in and of itself—a wonderful, healing, esteem-boosting role. This new role provides real-life confirmation to you that you are worthwhile, that the healthy risks you take can change your life for the better, and that you can and will make a difference in the world.

One of the best ways to start experiencing social success is to have someone who can witness the truth of your situation—and remind you of your value and strength as a human being. This entails finding at least one person in your life who stands by you and believes in you, especially when you have lost the capacity to believe in yourself. We all need people like this in our lives, someone who

---

[18] For more on this see: L. Mosher and V. Hendrix (2004). *Soteria: Through Madness to Deliverance*. Bloomington: Xlibris.

continually sends us a message of hope, even when all seems lost. A person like this on our side can be the beginning of a whole new way of life.

Your witness can be a family member, a friend, someone from church or a support group, a teacher, a peer who has also been diagnosed, or even a therapist. And there is certainly nothing wrong with having multiple witnesses in your life! When contacting mental health professionals, however, we urge you to stay away from those who tell you or your family that you have a broken brain or defective genetics or are doomed to a mental disorder for life. Research (not to mention our own personal experience) shows this is not true, and it is certainly not the message you need to heal.[19]

Healing can happen, and the more your shame evaporates the more opportunities you give your recovery.

Questions for Self-Reflection

1) In what ways do I currently feel ashamed or stigmatized in my life?
2) When did I first feel shame?
3) Do I or have I ever felt ashamed of myself in my family?
4) What would I be like as a person if I felt no shame or stigma?
5) In what areas of my life, past or present, do I feel no shame or stigma?
6) Who are the people in my life who respect and understand me the most, both in my family and outside my family?
7) What do I feel are my best qualities?

---

[19] See Jay Joseph's books, some of the best scientific books on the subject of the lack of evidence on genes being behind psychiatric disorders: 1) Joseph, J. (2004). *The Gene Illusion: Genetic Research in Psychiatry and Psychology Under the Microscope*. New York: Algora Publishing. 2) Joseph, J. (2006). *The Missing Gene: Psychiatry, Heredity, and the Fruitless Search for Genes*. New York: Algora Publishing.

Chapter 6

Your Relationship with the Mental Health System

Your contact with the mental health system likely began at the most difficult time in your life. You were vulnerable. A breakdown had just occurred. Your nerves were shot. Your anxiety was incredibly intense. You wondered if these feelings would ever end. Perhaps your thoughts were out of your control. Perhaps you were terrified. Perhaps you were even suicidal. You wanted help, and yet everything you tried had failed. Where did you turn?

Maybe you were lucky and found the mental health system empathic and nurturing. Perhaps you entered the office of a wise and compassionate clinician who didn't label you, and instead sought to understand the nature of your conflicts in order to help you resolve them. Some people enter the mental health system in this way, but unfortunately it seems they are quite the minority. Many have a very different experience—and mostly this chapter will deal with this all-too-common and less-than-stellar experience.

Perhaps you went to the emergency room, or perhaps to the office of a psychiatrist or therapist. Perhaps your family took you there—or even forced you to go. Perhaps upon arrival you were given a brief assessment and then a diagnosis—something with a rather unpleasant-sounding name that you probably wouldn't want to share with your friends or acquaintances, or maybe even with your parents. Rarely did it feel good to be diagnosed with "schizophrenia, paranoid subtype" or "bipolar disorder, most recent episode manic" or "major depression with psychotic features." And then there were all the official codes now associated with you, like 295.30, or 296.4, or 296.34. It all can seem so formal and foreboding and strange. Did these labels and codes become the new *You*?

The most private parts of yourself, your innermost thoughts and feelings, somehow became wrapped up into a neat label. It was like someone rewrote your whole life's story for you. It is not uncommon for people in this position to now ask questions about their identity, such as, "Who am I, then?" or "Were those thoughts me or were they the disorder?" People will sometimes make the disorder a fundamental part of their identity, saying, "I'm Bipolar" or "I'm Schizoaffective" or "I'm a Schizophrenic."

The fact is, even if your diagnosis might say something *about* you (though it also might not), *you are not your disorder!* No matter what anyone says, you are much, much more than that. And it can be a challenge to separate your real identity from the one the mental health system, and perhaps your family, is now attaching to you.

True Diagnosis Versus Convenient Labeling

There is a vast difference between true diagnosis and a convenient psychiatric label. True diagnosis, which tries to figure out what the real problem is, can never be summed up in a few words or a numeric code. True diagnosis involves mutual understanding and open, honest conversation in an ongoing human relationship, therapeutic or non-therapeutic. True diagnosis looks at deeper causes and keeps the idea of real recovery ever in mind.

Labeling, on the other hand, is impersonal. Labeling happens when some mental health professional unknown to you looks at some notes or asks you or a family member a series of questions about your life and then comes up with a diagnosis to pin on you. Unfortunately, the present-day hospital environment is set up such that the mental health professionals who work there have to make quick assessments and do not have the luxury of developing an ongoing, healing relationship. Labeling may be helpful to the hospital staff and the insurance companies, but it can be alienating and demeaning for you, especially when what you need most is understanding—and support.

People who get diagnosed with a mental disorder or are hospitalized are faced with the dilemma of what to tell current and future employers, coworkers, schools, and teachers about their situation. People have fears like, "What if my boss finds out that I've been hospitalized?" or "If I tell co-workers about what happened, what will they think?" Others think to themselves, "If I tell my friends I was diagnosed with a major psychiatric disorder they might never take me seriously again—and might reject me." These are real and valid concerns.

The bottom line is that you are not obligated to tell anyone what happened to you. Your privacy is an important and fundamental right. For this reason, many people choose to "camouflage" themselves, that is, keep hidden that they are or were diagnosed with a mental disorder. This is totally understandable and respectable. After all, since you are not your diagnosis, why should you be forced to share it with anyone—and especially with others who might think you are?

Unfortunately, many recovered people "camouflage" themselves too—and thus no one learns of their successes. Mostly we hear about the people who don't succeed, because they make the news and form the statistics that everyone quotes. A recovered person, on the other hand, makes the ultimate role model for people in the throes of a mental problem, yet if he or she remains "camouflaged" he or she cannot be a role model. Recovered people are everywhere, living "normal," day-to-day lives to the point that you would never know their history of having been in the mental health system. And the greatest irony is that few *psychiatrists* even know of their existences! No wonder then that most psychiatrists do not believe that people can recover fully from things like schizophrenia and bipolar disorder. They've simply never seen it before themselves.

Other people, though, feel a sense of relief from getting a psychiatric diagnosis, and might think to themselves, "Finally, what I've been going through actually has a name!"[20] But does this name actually mean anything? It may describe certain things you are experiencing or have experienced, but it doesn't tell anything about what caused a serious problem or what will help to cure it. In fact, the modern mental health system often has little or nothing to do with curing it, and instead just seeks to "manage" it—and manage you. In the recent past, many people with mental disorders were kept locked up in psych wards for years or decades, given electroshock, or even lobotomized. Few of these people got well. Nowadays basically everyone is prescribed medication—and some are forced to take it—be they antipsychotic medications, mood stabilizers, anti-anxiety medications, or antidepressants. Many people are prescribed a combination.

The problem is, these medications don't cure anything either. They are symptom suppressants, and sometimes don't even do that

---

[20] Joanne Greenberg shares of this experience in her chapter in this book. (See Chapter 20.)

effectively.[21] Although some people find great benefit and comfort from these medications, and find themselves allowed to return to work and school and relationships, others find that medications make the problems worse. And, on top of that, many of the medications risk causing serious medical problems, like diabetes, heart disease, obesity, and Parkinsonian-like symptoms, to name a few.[22]

Interestingly, some recent research on what is considered to be the most severe mental disorder, schizophrenia, suggests the possibility that people might be *more* likely to recover fully if they are *not* prescribed medication.[23] In fact, the World Health Organization studies have shown that people are *less likely to recover* from schizophrenia if they live in the United States (or other developed countries), where nearly everyone gets medicated, than they are if they live in third-world Africa or India, where almost no one gets medication because the medications are too expensive![24]

Some medications have disabling or dangerous side effects that are known and documented, and others have effects that haven't yet been documented or are known but hidden from the consumer. Pharmaceutical companies are under massive pressure to sell their products and keep up their profits, and sometimes behave unethically when it comes to disclosing medications' side effects, and even unhelpfulness. Many promote mental disorders as "illnesses" that you will have for life—"illnesses" that *require* their drugs.[25]

Perhaps your family believes this too, even derives comfort from

---

[21] R. Foltz (2008). "The Experience of Being Medicated in Schizophrenia: A Subjective Inquiry and Implications for Psychotherapy," pp. 159-173, in Garfield, D. and Mackler, D. (2008), *Beyond Medication: Therapeutic Engagement and the Recovery from Psychosis*. East Sussex, UK: Routledge. See also: 1) Jackson, G. (2005). *Rethinking Psychiatric Drugs: A Guide for Informed Consent*. Bloomington, IN: Author House. 2) Breggin, P. (1991). *Toxic Psychiatry*. New York: St. Martin's Press.

[22] G. Jackson (2005). *Rethinking Psychiatric Drugs: a Guide for Informed Consent*. Bloomington, IN.: Author House.

[23] M. Harrow and T. Jobe, "Factors involved in outcome and recovery in schizophrenia patients not on antipsychotic medications: a 15-year multifollow-up study." *The Journal of Nervous and Mental Disease*, May, 2007, 195(5): 406-14.

[24] See Robert Whitaker's groundbreaking book, *Mad in America*. [Whitaker, R. (2002). *Mad in America*. Cambridge, MA: Perseus Press.]

[25] See Eli Lilly's website for their popular antipsychotic, Zyprexa: www.zyprexa.com. See also Janssen's Website for their antipsychotic, Risperdal: www.risperdal.com.

believing it. You may feel a lot of pressure from them to get on medication—and stay on it. Many hold the idea that a pill will fix everything. Perhaps they have observed that you seem more stable when you are on your medications, and are less stable, or more prone to conflict, when you are off them.

But does this mean that your medication is therefore good for you—or necessary? Perhaps not. A healthy, gentle, nurturing living situation and lifestyle, which we discuss in detail in Chapter 10, can be more beneficial than medication, even in the short-term. The trick here is getting the people who care about you to stop worrying about you—meaning, that your behavior is no longer alarming them. If you can succeed in this task for an extended period of time, you will discover that the whole issue of medications simply ceases to come up.

Unfortunately, many people who stop taking their medications do so dangerously—without tapering gradually. Instead, they stop their medication abruptly, which radically throws off the neurotransmitters in the brain, and really *can* lead to psychosis—often a psychosis that was worse than any psychosis with which the people may have had initially.[26] Studies have also shown that you can take a non-psychotic person, put him or her on medications that deplete neurotransmitters in the same way that antipsychotics do, and then *make him or her literally psychotic* by withdrawing the medication abruptly![27]

The key, if you are going to stop taking your medication, is to do so *very, very slowly*, over a period of many months or years, with the help of a doctor. Many people do it without a doctor, and do not go slowly enough—and risk experiencing even worse problems than when they started!

Optimally, your decision of whether or not to take psychiatric medication—or for how long to take it and how to safely stop taking it—is a question to discuss with a psychiatrist whom you have come to know and trust. But at a more basic level, it is a deeply personal decision, and you deserve the final say in your treatment. Just as we

---

[26] Moncrieff, J (2006). Does antipsychotic withdrawal provoke psychosis? Review of the literature on rapid onset psychosis (supersensitivity psychosis) and withdrawal-related relapse. *Acta Psychiatrica Scandinavica*, 114(1): 3-13.

[27] This phenomenon, known as "supersensitivity psychosis," is discussed on pages 229-230 of G. Jackson's book *Rethinking Psychiatric Drugs: A Guide for Informed Consent.* [2005, Bloomington, IN: Author House.]

all have a right to our own private thoughts and feelings, we have a right to decide what we put into our bodies.[28]

Questions for Self-Reflection

1) What has been my overall experience with the mental health system?
2) How has the mental health system helped and empowered me?
3) How has the mental health system hurt me and led to disempowerment?
4) Does my diagnosis help me make sense of my experience or does it make me feel misunderstood?
5) What would be my ideal relationship with the mental health system?
6) Have I taken psychiatric medication, and if so, how, if at all, have they helped me? How, if at all, have they hurt me?
7) Do I believe it is possible for me to recover fully from whatever mental health or emotional problems I might have?

---

[28] For more on coming off psychiatric drugs, we recommend The Icarus Project's "Harm Reduction Guide to Coming Off Psychiatric Drugs." It was written by Will Hall, who contributed Chapter 19 of this book. We also recommend the book *Coming Off Psychiatric Medication*, edited by Peter Lehmann (2004, Shrewsbury, UK, Peter Lehmann Publishing). Another good resource is the website *www.comingoff.com*.

Chapter 7

Boundaries: The Basis for Respect

Families who have a member diagnosed with a psychiatric disorder often, though not always, have boundary issues—which may both contribute to a mental problem *and* result from it. The word "boundaries" gets thrown around a lot these days, and it is important to make clear what we mean when we say it. Boundaries are the invisible walls around our personhood, the borders of our sense of self. We have physical boundaries, which include our bodies, our clothing, and our pain thresholds, which others must respect if they wish not to physically abuse us. We also have sexual boundaries, which family members are expected not to cross. And we have emotional boundaries, which are the most subtle to define, and, as such, the easiest to disrespect. Our boundaries are inherent in our rights as human beings. When others cross our boundaries they violate our humanity.

People diagnosed with a psychiatric disorder have often experienced extreme histories of boundary violations in their childhood families. Perhaps their parents experienced the same in their childhood histories, and have not resolved them—and thus have repeated them unconsciously with their children, to one degree or another. This can be very difficult for parents and children alike to acknowledge, because who wants to see that they abuse, or were abused by, the people they love most in the world, and were most entrusted to love?

For instance, many studies show that people diagnosed with psychiatric disorders were much more likely to have been sexually abused by family members than people who never get labeled with a mental disorder.[29] Likewise, people with a history of a psychiatric

---

[29] J. Read, P. Fink, T. Rudegeair, V. Felitti, C. Whitfield (2008). "Child Maltreatment and Psychosis: A Return to a Genuinely Integrated Bio-Psycho-Social Model." *Clinical Schizophrenia and Related Psychoses.* October, 2008: 235-254.

disorder are more likely to have been physically and emotionally abused—and neglected.[30] Many people with such histories of boundary violations—especially those who don't recognize that these *were in fact boundary violations*—carry these behavior patterns into adulthood, unconsciously perpetuating the cycle of staying victims, and sometimes equally unconsciously becoming perpetrators.[31]

Your job, if you are to improve your relationships with your family, is to strengthen your boundaries—and to learn to respect theirs better. This is no easy feat, because strong boundaries may not have been the greatest skill of your family. But boundaries are never too late to learn—and practice. Some boundaries are easier to see clearly, and defend properly. For instance, putting a stop to overt sexual abuse, though very difficult in some cases, is clear and straightforward enough, because in the eyes of the public, at least, sexual abuse is universally unacceptable.

However, covert, subtle sexual abuse—especially in the emotional realm—is much harder to detect and to root out. Sometimes parents tell children things that are sexually inappropriate, or share their nudity in inappropriate ways, or share inappropriately sexual reading or visual material, or simply become far too involved in their children's romantic or sexual lives. Yet often this can be considered normal and healthy by the family—even by society—and sometimes both parent and child are actually, to a degree, addicted to it. It forms their sense of "loving" one another, even though there really is little that is loving about it. Many parents get their romantic or love needs met through you, their child, instead of through other consensual, age-appropriate adults. They may have never put an inappropriate hand on you, but they may still have committed a radical boundary violation—which devastated your development. And on the other

---

[30] Again, see: J. Read, P. Fink, T. Rudegeair, V. Felitti, C. Whitfield (2008). "Child Maltreatment and Psychosis: A Return to a Genuinely Integrated Bio-Psycho-Social Model." *Clinical Schizophrenia and Related Psychoses.* October, 2008: 235-254.

[31] The writer Alice Miller explains this dynamic beautifully in many of her works, and we cannot recommend them highly enough. See these books of hers for further information on healing childhood wounds, as opposed to repeating them and passing them on: 1) *The Drama of the Gifted Child* (1997, New York: Basic Books). 2) *Thou Shalt Not Be Aware* (1984, New York: Farrar, Straus, and Giroux). 2) *Banished Knowledge* (1990, New York: Doubleday). 4) *For Your Own Good* (1987, Farrar, Straus, and Giroux).

hand, many grown adults still get their deepest love needs met from their parents—and never realize how inappropriate it is.

Your job is to figure out what boundaries and behaviors are appropriate *for you*—and what are not. Although the process of setting and enforcing boundaries often takes a lot of work, the results can actually be very rewarding—and relieving. But where do you start in terms of setting better boundaries?

Let's say you decide that you no longer wish to tolerate people talking to you in a tone that makes you feel bad or criticized. Perhaps your first step will involve planning what to do or say the next time this happens. This is where you can be creative. Perhaps you can decide to simply leave the room, or perhaps you might prepare a statement, such as "don't take that kind of tone with me." Or you might decide to put your hand gently on the other person's shoulder and say "ouch, that hurts me." There is no right or wrong here, no best or worst way, and more than likely you will have to take different approaches with different people.

Next, you have to be brave enough to put the gears of your decision into motion when the actual situation occurs. Be gentle with yourself here: it might take a few times of getting swept up in the emotion of the situation before you find the presence of mind to take the plunge—and take action. This can be terrifying. Perhaps it will work successfully—and perhaps it will not. Sometimes our decisions to change our behavior and set new boundaries, especially with family members, can meet a lot of resistance. It can even cause backlash against you. We do not promise that setting new boundaries is easy—but it often does change things.

Perhaps it will take a few tries before the other person recognizes your new boundaries. Or perhaps they will recognize and respect your new boundary right away—or perhaps not at all. Regardless, after you have laid down the boundary to the best of your ability, you can take a step back, spend some time alone with yourself, and appreciate how *you* acted differently. And depending on how they respond, you can decide for yourself how you wish to move forward in the relationship.

Overall, sorting out new boundaries is more easily said than done, and takes much self-study—perhaps years of it. In the spirit of self-study, we offer a list of family behaviors that are often laden with boundary violations. As you read the following list, you might assess if you feel your family relationships involve boundary problems in any of these areas. Each family, however, is different, and as you read this list we urge you not to jump to conclusions too quickly about boundary violations.

Family Behaviors That Are Often Laden with Boundary Violations

- Any violence in the home, including corporal punishment toward children.

  > *Note: Although some cultures consider spanking children to be an important tool of child-rearing, we disagree. In this regard, some Scandinavian countries have wisely made it a crime to spank children.*

- Children staying too close to their parents at the expense of developing independent lives and strong friendships.
- A parent and child being "best friends."

  > *Note: The difference in power between parent and child, even an adult child, is often too great to make friendship between parent and child appropriate. For this reason we encourage both parents and children to develop friendships with peers.*

- Therapeutic or pseudo-therapeutic relationships between parents and children.

  > *Note: Often it is safer for parents to mind their own business, support their children emotionally in other ways, and let their children learn to work out their own problems in other, independent ways*

- Parents and children sharing the same bed.

  > *Note: We recognize that in some cultures this can have a very different meaning that it does in Western cultures, and as such we do not consider bed-sharing to be an inherent boundary violation.*

- Breastfeeding children past a certain age.
- Parental nudity in the home—and child nudity past a certain young age. Although some cultures experience nudity in

a healthier way, in an over-sexualized society such as ours, nudity and sexuality are so strongly tied together that it often renders nudity inappropriate in the home.
- Parents regularly fighting or arguing in front of children. This can be extremely psychologically traumatizing for a child, especially a young child.
- Yelling and screaming of all varieties.

> *Note: High emotional intensity can be especially disruptive to people diagnosed with psychiatric disorders, and may cause preexisting problems to spiral out of control.*

- Cruel verbal language. We have often observed people who "hear voices"—especially cruel, self-hating voices—share their experiences of having been treated to verbal cruelty in their childhoods that is remarkably similar to the "voices" they now hear.[32]
- Racist or sexist attitudes.
- Alcoholism or drug abuse.

> *Note: Alcohol and drugs tends to weaken family boundaries further. So much sexual abuse and violence happens when there is parental alcoholism involved.*

- Parents regularly borrowing money from their children.
- Parents financially "bailing out" children for financial problems or errors.

> *Note: It is often the case that being extremely helpful to a "troubled" child can seem like love, whereas in reality this form of "loving" can be crippling—and can further enable the problem.*

---

[32] Recent scientific study, however, suggests that not all "voice hearing" is pathological—and that sometimes it is just a normal part of human variation, and can even be psychologically healthy or helpful for some people. As noted in psychologist Gail Hornstein's book *Agnes's Jacket*, recent studies in the United Kingdom suggest that a sizeable percentage of the population heard voices, and most of them had never been diagnosed with a psychiatric problem or been in the mental health system in any way. In fact, they were considered perfectly "normal." [See Hornstein, G. (2009). *Agnes's Jacket: A Psychologist's Search for the Meanings of Madness*. New York: Rodale.]

- Parents sharing credit cards with adult children. We encourage adults to learn to become financially independent. (For more on the subject of dealing with money, see Chapter 11 of this book.)
- Parents becoming over-involved, controlling, or simply too curious about their children's friendships or romantic relationships. This is private material, and often best kept that way!
- Parental nagging or unrelenting criticism.

  > *Note: Many parents justify their nagging and criticism as something helpful to their child, or something their child needs. In reality, this parental behavior is usually a sign of the parent's frustration and anger, and risks being the opposite of helpful.*

- Parents choosing their children's clothing past a certain age.
- Parents constantly intervening in their children's conflicts—especially their adult children's conflicts.

  > *Note: How can you get strong if you can't learn to solve your own problems?*

- Adult children regularly asking parents for personal advice. We recommend seeking out advice from independent sources.
- Parents discussing marital problems with their children.
- Any manipulations and ultimatums.
- Parents having difficulties setting healthy limits.

  > *Note: Ultra-tolerant or ultra-liberal parents are often the flip side of the coin of ultra-rigid or ultra-conservative parents... Both risk being unhelpful.*

- Any teasing, mocking, or putting down of one another.
- Parents commenting on their children's sexual attractiveness—or lack of sexual attractiveness. This can often be a subtle form of sexual abuse.
- People entering private rooms (including bathrooms) without knocking.

> *Note: Although many families consider this behavior to be normal, in many cases it sets up a dynamic where people don't feel their have any safe, private space of their own.*

- Over-tickling (and any tickling at all past a very young age).

  > *Note: Tickling often disguises hostility—or even sexuality.*

- Parents doing their children's homework.

  > *Note: As the saying goes, "give a man a fish, and he eats for a day, but teach a man to fish and he eats for the rest of his life..."*

- Parents monitoring their adult child's psychiatric medication in cases where this monitoring is unwanted.
- Forcing or pressuring children to accept certain religious beliefs or behaviors.
- Parents sharing their life's woes, and their grief processes, with their children.
- Chronic lateness, either by parents or children.
- Gossip of all varieties.
- Parents doing the laundry for their adult children.

We hope you just take this list as a guideline for deeper exploration, and self-study—not as "The Law." Although it might appear that we are "banning" a certain degree of family behavior that many families consider normal, and throwing everything into the pot of "boundary violations," this is not our intention. We are not Puritans. We are simply aware how easy it is to disrespect one another, and how negative the effects of this disrespect can be. Instead we just suggest keeping an open mind when looking at family behavior, and questioning the degree to which boundary violations might exist.

Ultimately, our job is to struggle to have better boundaries—and thus better family respect, and ultimately better self-respect. When we work toward developing healthier relationships with one another, we do ourselves, and our relationships in the family, a good turn.

Questions for Self-Reflection

1) What are the strengths and weaknesses in my boundaries?
2) How have my boundaries changed over time?
3) In what ways are boundaries within my family appropriate versus inappropriate?
4) How appropriate were my family's and my own boundaries when I was a child?
5) How are my boundaries different in my relationships with people *outside my family* than with my family members?
6) In what ways can I improve my boundaries with my family members?
7) How might my life be different if I had better boundaries?

Chapter 8

Dealing with Anger, Frustration, and Grief

People who end up in the mental health system, especially those diagnosed with a serious psychiatric disorder, have experienced much loss—and have a lot to be angry about. Hopes have been dashed, dreams shattered, progress squelched, self-esteem eroded, boundaries violated, and autonomy dissipated. Anyone who has been though this would be expected to have a reaction, and often your family, being closest to you, bears the brunt of it.

You may feel they are responsible for some of your misery, but the degree to which this is true is a secondary point in your relationship with them. The primary point is managing your feelings in a way that best benefits *you*. If you are in heavy conflict with them, and are expressing your anger, rage, frustration, or grief toward them, and they have *any* degree of control over your life, you are setting yourself up for only more trouble, more pain, more loss, and more frustration—and less control.

Fighting with parents can become an endless loop—a classic vicious cycle. Although it can be temporarily gratifying to rage at them, argue with them, debate with them, scream at them, express your hurt to them, try to get them to apologize, and try to prove them wrong, generally what we really seek when we do these things is love and understanding. Behind all the rage, and sometimes even behind violence, is sadness, and behind the sadness is *need*—and hope for rescue. If most people could be deeply honest, what they would probably say to their parents is this: "Mom, Dad, I am horribly hurt about what I have gone through, and I feel lost and confused and don't know how to break out of the rut I'm in. And I'm furious at both of you because you're not helping me! Can't you help me get what I need? Please, love me in the way I need to be loved—*finally!*"

The problem is, your parents are probably just as confused as you. If they knew what to do, chances are they would do it—or would have done it *years before*. They are stuck in their own unconscious ruts. These ruts control them and control their perspective, and the more you push them and have conflict with them the less they have the ability to take back their own control and grow toward a more helpful and useful perspective.

Your job is figure out how to take back your own self-control. And again, this challenge is easier said than done. Is the solution simply to stop fighting with them? This may not be possible, because your degree of hurt and sadness and rage is just too huge to put back in a hidden box in the recesses of your personality. You have probably learned by now that squelching or burying your feelings generally only leads to worse misery—and more problems. Sometimes letting it out, even letting it out on the wrong people in the wrong ways at the wrong volume, just plain feels better.

So the bigger question is how to let your feelings out in appropriate ways. It is safest to find someone *outside* your family to be able to share things with, someone with whom you have a relationship that is less loaded down with historical patterns, buried hurts, flashing memories, and scorching words. The next chapter deals with this in detail. For now, though, we will say that it is rare that much gets resolved through direct, unmediated family conflict.

The goal is to be able to grieve your losses and your wounds, as opposed to acting them out. Grief is a complex process, involving not just the crying and tears we associate with mourning, but also anger and rage. The key is using discretion as you go through your grief process. Unlike the powerful feelings that initially come through the drama of overt family conflict, grieving makes you emotionally vulnerable in a whole different way. When you grieve, life offers you the opportunity to acknowledge your surfacing feelings in silence and privacy. You get to sit with them, feel them, study them, and explore them—and ultimately pass through them. But again, most of all you get the opportunity to sit with them and feel them. And sometimes they last a long, long time.

There are no two ways around it: grieving is a lengthy process, and one in which you remain emotionally vulnerable for a long time. This can seem much like depression—and sometimes grieving does overlap with depression. The difference is, depression is stuckness; grieving moves forward. Depression involves a broad feeling of hopelessness and helplessness. Grieving involves making discriminations between what has truly been lost and is gone forever, and what still exists and still offers hope. Depression is like a stagnant pond full of algae, muck, and pollution. Grieving is a clean mountain lake that allows you to see right to the bottom.

But what is the difference between grieving family conflict and *acting it out?*

The main difference is that *acting out* family conflict doesn't *make* you vulnerable, rather, it *leaves* you vulnerable. It's easy to feel all-powerful in the middle of a fit of rage, or even a fit of violence, which is why we may be tempted in this direction—and why very young and frustrated children love temper tantrums. But in reality you are only setting yourself to be further crushed. When you scream and yell and throw things, even hit people, you not only make enemies—perhaps even enemies of your own family—but make enemies who have just the evidence they need to take even more control away from you. You become that much closer to ending up back in the hospital, or on higher doses of medication, or possibly even in jail. And you will likely end up with massive regrets—from having hurt yourself *and* those you love.

Losing your self-control—and handing this control over to others—only prolongs the inevitable grief that will be required to help you work through your deeper conflicts. You need as much self-control as possible to be able to grieve. It's hard enough to grieve *with* self-control, *and virtually impossible without it.*

Grief is a private process. The only interaction that happens in grief is between *you and yourself*—between the best and most self-loving sides of you and the most wounded and hurt and confused and needy sides of you. Others can help guide you through grief, but ultimately it is an internal job.

When you grieve you give yourself the greatest gift. Many people who have been diagnosed with a major psychiatric disorder stopped giving themselves emotional gifts a long time ago. The only gifts they give themselves are Trojan Horses, the dubious gifts of harshness, pushiness, self-flagellation, self-criticism, and instant gratification. These only anchor you deeper into misery.

Most have even forgotten the concept of self-love, because they have lived so long with self-hatred, self-doubt, and, worst of all, sometimes even a lack of any relationship with a self. Many people have truly forgotten that even they have a self. Thus they have forgotten their basic responsibility to themselves: to nurture themselves.

Self-love is a wonderful place to start on the grieving process.

Once you become an adult it is no longer appropriate for your parents to be your primary source of love. On the other hand, it's terribly hard to love yourself after a breakdown, after so many painful years, and perhaps after so many years without an external model or template of others loving you. But you can try. We encourage you to try to be kind to yourself—and gentle with yourself in your thoughts and actions. Just recognizing this as a goal can go a long way toward healing—and bringing balance back into your relationship with your family.

Like all things on the healing process, it is difficult. But there is hope.

Questions for Self-Reflection

1) What are some of the losses I have suffered in my life—including in relation to my psychiatric diagnosis or mental health history?
2) In what ways am I angry about these losses I have suffered?
3) To what degree have I grieved these losses?
4) What resentments do I hold toward family members because of my losses?
5) To what degree do I feel they or I am responsible for my problems—and responsible for solving them?
6) In what ways do I act out my anger, both within my family and beyond my family?
7) How much energy do I put into making myself a stronger, healthier person?
8) In what ways do I love myself?

Chapter 9

Forgiveness

Many spiritual and psychological leaders counsel that practicing forgiveness is the key to healing old wounds, and suggest that those who cannot forgive can never live in peace. This is partially true, and partially untrue. Practicing forgiveness may not be immediately appropriate when people have more serious or pressing emotional problems. Forgiveness is instead a long-term consequence of grieving and healing ancient wounds, and people who attempt to forgive others too quickly often bypass or shortchange their own grieving process.

People do not develop serious emotional problems, to the point of psychosis, for no reason. Often psychosis develops in the context of conflicted and faulty human relationships. This can be within the family and outside it in the larger world, or both. Sometimes serious problems develop in the context of abuse, and sometimes this involves serious abuse, be it emotional, physical, or sexual. And sometimes it is very hard to know why a person's problems developed. The reasons are complex, multi-layered, and often hidden from view. And when we consider how painful these reasons usually are, we can understand why there is a lot of incentive to block them out—and even forget them. There is a reason people block out memories of their traumas for years and even decades—and sometimes for a lifetime.

As we stated in the last chapter, ancient wounds need time to heal. When people do heal their wounds they spontaneously forgive those who caused them the abuse. They do not forget their abuse—in fact, they remember it better than ever, because they no longer have any need to block it out—and they do not necessarily want to spend time with those who abused them, but they are able to let go of their rage, their anger, their bitterness, and their resentment. And usually this process of letting go takes a long, long time.

One problem, however, is that the people who caused the damage, especially if they are close family members, would sometimes prefer to be forgiven quickly. Forgiveness eases *their* mind and can bring a whole family a measure of quick peace and seeming comfort. But that doesn't mean it helps the recovery of the person with the most serious problems, the person with the psychosis or the psychiatric diagnosis. Often it actually hurts him or her. But sometimes this is a compromise that person is willing to accept. In fact, at times a certain family member can be designated, in an unspoken way, to play the role of the person who practices instant forgiveness for the sake of family peace.

But what are the consequences of instant, premature forgiveness?

The consequences are that the person who has prematurely forgiven fails to get a chance to work through his sadness, his rage, and his resentments. He has to keep quiet, even to himself, about what's really going on beneath his surface, about what's on his mind, and about his deepest feelings. He has to bury them—for the sake of instant peace. In some ways this is not unlike the tranquilizing effect of antipsychotic medications. They suppress the deeper symptoms, but do not cure the problem—and often create a whole spate of problems of their own.

It is true, though, that practicing premature forgiveness might feel good in the short-run. It seems that the person doing the forgiveness has healed and looks so much happier, and also brings more comfort and happiness to those around him. But he risks living forever with the potential that his deeper truth—the truth of his squelched feelings—will someday erupt and send him right back to square one.

For this reason it is far better that he not forgive anyone for anything they did to him until he is fully ready—in his own time. No one can tell him when he is ready, and often *he himself* might want to be ready sooner than he is really able. After all, there is much pressure on him to "get over the anger," "look normal," "quit being so bitter," and to "just choose happiness for a change!"

But maybe his anger and rage and bitterness are perfectly healthy and appropriate, considering what he has been through, not just in his earliest life, but in the psychiatric system as well. Many people have been terribly traumatized by the psychiatric system *even after they had serious emotional problems*, and it would never be appropriate to expect them to forgive until they, and only they, felt fully ready.

But then there are others among us—and perhaps we all do this to some degree—who hold our resentments against people who never really damaged us, or minimally damaged us. We do this for many reasons, including to protect ourselves from the pain of knowing what our most serious traumas are, to keep a family or social balance in order, and to feel we've forgiven those we love who damaged us. We take out our anger and rage against innocent or relatively innocent others, and refuse to forgive them for things *they may have never even really done to us!* Sometimes it is simply easier and more convenient to forgive the most abusive people and refuse to forgive the less abusive ones. After all, it can be very painful to acknowledge the wrongs that those we love have done to us—especially since this acknowledgment can be very disruptive to a family.

A great example of this is the enraged sexual abuse survivor who feels no direct anger toward his actual abusers, and actually feels he has forgiven them, but lashes out in near-constant rage and cursing bitterness at fellow drivers on the road—for driving too fast, driving too slow, cutting him off in traffic, and sometimes simply for existing. What he is really doing, however, is diverting his rage away from his real traumatizers and onto the wrong people. This makes it impossible for him to heal, and to come to a genuine state of forgiveness, because you can't heal if you keep blaming the wrong people.

But is blame healthy? It would seem from all we read that it is not.

Sometimes it is. And sometimes it isn't. Clearly blaming the wrong people is not, nor is blaming the right people if you hold an expectation that they will rescue you from your pain. They cannot rescue you. Nothing but grieving and taking personal responsibility can rescue you from your pain and traumas.

But often blame *is* a part of the healing process. The question then is what is a healthy way to blame—versus an unhealthy way. The healthy side of blame is holding the right people responsible and accountable for the actual damages they did to you. The unhealthy side of blame is failing to take personal responsibility yourself for fixing those damages—and expecting them to fix it. They cannot. You can.

This is the best part of being an adult: you have the power to take responsibility for yourself, and make healthy changes in your life.

Two things we have observed that allow people to grieve, to practice blame in a healthy way, and ultimately to forgive are as follows: *time and distance*. Both of these really do allow for the healing of old wounds. We have already addressed time—the years and decades it takes. Distance is more complex. It can be very hard to grieve and forgive adequately if there is too much closeness. The survivor of a brutal crime cannot be expected to forgive the criminal who assaulted her while she remains in close proximity to him. Nor can a psychiatric survivor be expected to forgive psychiatric workers or therapists who traumatized her while she remains hospitalized by them and under their control.

For this reason, it is often healthiest, and most beneficial for the ultimate goal of recovery, to take distance from those toward whom we hold deep bitterness. This gives us the space to explore our feelings in a safer and less pressured environment. It also allows us to get perspective—the chance to take in the bigger picture.

Others say, however, that the best thing to help you forgive is to understand *why* those who wounded you did what they did. They suggest that you study their pasts, empathize with them, and learn about intergenerational patterns of abuse and trauma. After all, certainly those who wounded you did what they did for a reason—because someone did similarly cruel and inappropriate things to them along the way.

But empathizing with those who wounded you can be very risky, and sometimes, if practiced prematurely, can thwart real recovery. Yes, those who traumatized or abused you were also traumatized and abused, but that doesn't let them off the hook for their actions, and doesn't heal what they did to you. Only grieving does. Before you empathize with those who traumatized you it is vital that you learn to empathize fully with yourself. Often this is much harder than forgiving one's abusers.[33] Forgiving traumatizers wins you the love of others, and people will say how mature you are, and how you're the "bigger person."

But real maturity comes with empathizing fully with yourself—first and foremost. When you can accomplish that, then forgiving everyone else, if that is what you wish, becomes a natural matter of course.

But how do you empathize with yourself?

This is the work of the whole healing process. Again, time and distance sometimes help, though the key is finding a healthy balance between distance and closeness. Some people find ways to maintain closeness without taking much distance, while others move far away

---

[33] See Alice Miller's classic book *Drama of the Gifted Child* (1997, New York: Basic Books) for more on this subject.

from those toward whom they are bitter. In the latter case, this can be painful, laden with homesickness and loneliness, but often, if they can find a good, nurturing, stable living situation from which to operate, it benefits them—and ultimately those toward whom they were bitter. A reconnection might take years, but had they never left home a real reconnection would probably never have happened at all.

Questions for Self-Reflection

1) Toward whom do I feel bitterness and resentment?
2) What is the cause of my bitterness and resentment?
3) Whom do I feel I have not yet forgiven?
4) Why do I feel I have not yet forgiven them?
5) Whom have I forgiven and why?
6) What do I feel would allow me to let go of these resentments?
7) Would letting go of my resentments toward them feel healthy or unhealthy for me in my recovery?
8) What are some ways I might be able to take healthy distance from those whom I cannot yet forgive?

Chapter 10

Practicing a Healthy Lifestyle

Nothing is more healing in life than practicing a healthy lifestyle. Often people who have been diagnosed with a major psychiatric disorder live unusually *unhealthy* lifestyles, in a variety of ways. And they may not even realize it, because unhealthiness has become so familiar and entrenched, sometimes to the degree that it is all they know. Taking steps toward a healthier lifestyle can actually feel extremely uncomfortable at first, and at times downright emotionally painful, even terrifying. It is the same for children who were raised on soda, candy, and potato chips: they generally hate switching to a diet of drinking milk and eating spinach and carrots, finding them disgusting to the taste.

But just as Rome wasn't built in a day, converting an unhealthy life to a healthy one doesn't happen overnight. And that's a blessing, because if it did, it would probably be too overwhelming. Gradual, gentle changes are easiest on the system. And after all, what's the rush? Life is long—and so is recovery and healing, as all the recovered contributors in this book will soon attest.

Practicing a healthy lifestyle can happen in many seemingly disconnected areas of your life. The connection between these different areas is *you*—your self-loving, dedicated, responsible relationship with yourself. Taking responsibility for yourself and your life's path is the key to empowerment.

Developing a Support Network

One excellent way to start developing a healthier lifestyle is to develop a support network outside your family. Many people have leaned on their family for emotional support for so long that they have become socially isolated. This puts massive pressure on the family and generally degrades the quality of family relationships. And, ironically, it even works *against* people getting any support from their families, because their families can become resentful, overburdened, and frustrated. On the other hand, when people step outside of their family for their support, everything begins to change.[34]

Perhaps you wish to make new friends. Sometimes this is very hard at first. Strangers may not be as accepting or welcoming as they should be—as we all know well. Perhaps you will try returning to old friends. But maybe they have moved on with their lives or no longer have room for you. This can be very painful, but do not despair. There are *always* places where people—good, caring, understanding people—are open to new friends. The question is finding those places—and allowing *yourself* to be open to letting someone new into *your* life. For many people, the process of being diagnosed with a psychiatric disorder and ending up "in the system" is a process of stripping away one's trust in others. Letting in a friend is the opposite—and perhaps the greatest risk any of us can take. The key is to be patient—and let life unfold. All important things take time.

There are other places to find support outside of your family. Maybe a support group can help. Many people find great relief and comfort—and even insight—sitting and talking with others who have issues or conflicts similar to their own. Or maybe a therapist or peer counselor can help. Sometimes professional or semi-professional help proves invaluable.[35] Someone who devotes himself or herself to your well-being in a focused and dedicated way can go a long way toward rebuilding your trust in humanity and your trust in yourself. You lost whatever trust you had for a good reason. Now life is trying to help you get it back. The key is that you listen to your inner voice of truth as you venture out into the world to expand your horizons.

Getting a Good Night's Sleep

Another key to a healthy lifestyle involves getting a good night's sleep—every night. It is amazing how many people diagnosed with

---

[34] See the chapters of Patch Adams (Chapter 21), David Oaks (Chapter 15), and Dorothy Dundas (Chapter 18) for more on the great value of stepping outside the family system to develop a social network.

[35] See Matthew Morrissey's, Dorothy Dundas's, and Joanne Greenberg's chapter (Chapters 17, 18, and 20 in this volume) for more on recovered people who derived great benefit from psychotherapy. We will discuss the benefits and dangers of psychotherapy in more detail in Chapter 11.

mental problems have incredibly erratic sleep patterns. Sometimes poor sleep patterns, as in the case of Matthew Morrissey (see Chapter 17), can even trigger a person's psychosis!

One night such a person might sleep three hours, the next night fifteen hours, and then he or she might miss two nights of sleep in a row—and then sleep two days straight. They may have no set bedtime, and sometimes their schedule has them staying up till sunrise every morning and waking up after the sun has already set. This puts them radically out of sync with the rest of the world—and contributes strongly to a feeling of isolation and internal frustration even within their family. Also, people who sleep erratically are often irritable, which contributes to imbalanced emotions and heightened family conflict.

We encourage people to go to sleep before midnight and get up in the morning, by nine o'clock—seven days a week. Keeping the same bedtime every night goes a long way toward bringing life back into balance. This clears the thought process more than any medication and is simple and natural, to boot. It also sets the stage for a productive, useful, health-oriented day—with sunshine, not artificial light. Sometimes people initially take medication to help them get their sleep back on track, but some good old-fashioned self-discipline does the trick just as well—or better—with no side effects. It's a lot harder to practice self-discipline than it is to pop a pill, but the feeling of well-being that comes from knowing you did it yourself, from within, is incomparable.

Considering the importance of getting a good night's sleep, we offer a few other tips for good "sleep hygiene":

1) Limit or end caffeine usage, especially in the afternoons and evenings.
2) Keep your bedroom dark, and your sleeping surface neither too hard nor too soft.
3) Remove distractions from your bedroom, so the focus there is sleep (i.e. remove television, computers, work desks, bills, etc.).
4) Exercise vigorously several hours before bed—but not too close to bedtime. Being nicely tired really does help with sleep.
5) Wake up at the same time every day. Very important!
6) Avoid eating or drinking, and, especially, eating heavy meals, before bedtime.

7) Avoid alcohol use, as it can seriously disrupt the sleep cycle.
8) If at all possible avoid the use of sleep medication, and if you do use them, then do so as sparingly as possible.
9) Use a white noise machine, as this can be very soothing, and blocks out extraneous sound.
10) Avoid intense emotional interaction in the late afternoons and evening—so your mind will be calmer before bedtime.
11) Try listening to soothing, relaxing music before bedtime—this helps some people prepare for a good night of sleep.

Changing Your Diet

Hand in glove with good sleep is good diet. It is all too common that people with mental problems, for various reasons, eat poorly. Yes, sometimes eating healthy is more expensive than eating poorly, but again, with focus and discipline, there are ways to accomplish just about anything. We address money issues in detail in the next chapter.

Meanwhile, eating a nutritious, well-balanced diet does the mind and body a great turn. But many people do not even know that they are eating a poor diet—and don't even realize that this is contributing to their emotional problems. Here it can help to talk to a nutritionist or dietician to learn the basics about diet, but also, if that proves difficult, a simple book on diet can always be found in the local library. And such information is readily available on the internet. And sometimes there are specific diets that might be particularly good for you.

Some general rules of thumb, however, are worth noting. More fruits and vegetables are good, and the produce section in the grocery store is your friend. Processed food is generally not so good, and often loaded with fats and salt and other things that tend to be dangerous, especially if you are overweight, have high blood pressure, or diabetes, which, sadly, seem to be becoming more and more of a problem in our modern world—and are known to come as a side effect of many of the new antipsychotic medications.

Also, it's always good to remember that "you are what you eat." With that in mind, why put unhealthy junk into your body? McDonald's might be easy and convenient, but they market their food to taste good, sell in massive quantities, and make them rich—*not to make you healthy*. In light of this, why not eat gentle, loving, balanced food? It might not taste as good at first, but the rewards you will reap will make it so worth your while.

Drugs and Alcohol

Although we do not want to overstate our case, and sound like a prudish "Grandma," our experience has shown us that drugs and alcohol are very emotionally risky in the lives of people trying to recover from serious emotional problems. Drugs and alcohol throw off the mental balance, and sometimes throw it off hard. Yes, sometimes they can bring on feelings of inner peace and euphoria and well-being, but these are only temporary, and usually create a backswing in the other direction. And the problems they create almost always outweigh the positives.

Drugs and alcohol are expensive, sometimes ridiculously expensive, especially for those on fixed incomes—or on no income at all. We have heard so many stories of people diagnosed with severe psychiatric disorders who spend their entire month's income on drugs or alcohol in a matter of days—and sometimes hours! How can such a person expect to lead a balanced life—or have balanced family relationships?

But perhaps most importantly, drugs and alcohol, even if taken moderately, change your self-perception. Although this can be pleasant or even euphoric for people who have an active aversion to themselves and are full of negative feelings and self-hatred, drugs and alcohol make it very hard to connect in an integrated way with the best of oneself. These substances also lower inhibitions, and the abuse of them causes people to do the most damaging things to their own lives, and often most dramatically within their family relationships. So much violence is committed while people are drunk or on drugs—and so many of the most cruel things are said by people when they are on mind-altering substances. Likewise, some people are triggered directly into psychosis by taking drugs. So much research has been done on the effects of marijuana on the mental state,[36] and suggest how many people might have avoided a psychotic break had they not smoked marijuana. And of course other drugs can do the same. Many are triggered into psychosis

---

[36] See: D. Fergusson, R. Poulton, P. Smith, and J. Boden (1996), "Cannabis and psychosis." British Medical Journal, 332, 172-175.

through the use of alcohol, cocaine, LSD, magic mushrooms, and other street drugs.[37]

We encourage people to try to go through life as drug-free and alcohol-free as possible. It's worked for us—and for many whom we have seen go on to do great things.

Some stop using drugs and alcohol on their own, others try Twelve Step Programs such as Alcoholics Anonymous and Narcotics Anonymous, and others seek professional help, even religious help. Any or all of these methods can help guide people toward an optimally balanced life. It's just a question of which route works best for you.

Getting Exercise

Many people diagnosed with psychiatric disorders gave up on exercise long ago—if they ever exercised at all. Their bodies are terribly out of shape, and many have become obese—sometimes as a secondary consequence of their psychiatric medications. Being overweight or out of shape is detrimental to both mind and body, and to spirit as well. It's depressing to sit around all day, and never get moving!

Some studies have shown that good, gentle exercise a few times a week is just as effective at combating depression as an antidepressant[38]—and we have witnessed the same with exercise in relation to more serious mental problems. And once you do start exercising, it feels great to see your body, which you may have long neglected, get back into shape. Your body is your temple: treat it well and you will feel a hundred times better. As such, we encourage you to take this facet of your recovery seriously.

There are many ways to exercise. The simplest way is to take walks—a nice, long walk several times a week. This becomes all the

---

[37] See David Oaks's chapter in this volume (Chapter 15) on the negative effect of marijuana on his emotional problems.

[38] M. Babyak, J. Blumenthal, S. Herman, P. Khatri, M. Doraiswamy, K. Moore, W. Craighead, T. Baldewicz, and K. Krishnan. "Exercise Treatment for Major Depression: Maintenance of Therapeutic Benefit at 10 Months." *Psychosomatic Medicine*, September/October 2000. *See also:* J. Blumenthal, M. Babyak, K. Moore, W. Craighead, S. Herman, P. Khatri, R. Waugh, M. Napolitano, L. Forman, M. Appelbaum, M. Doraiswamy, K. Krishnan. "Effects of Exercise Training on Older Patients With Major Depression." *Archives of Internal Medicine*, October 25, 1999.

more enjoyable if you have a friend or acquaintance to walk with—and talk with. This makes for wonderful interaction, and gets you out of the house and out into the world—and into the fresh air. It breaks the cycle of compulsively watching television or staying glued to the internet. It gets your blood circulating, your heart beating, your mind flowing, and your healthy chemicals pumping through your brain. It gives you a new perspective on things, and almost universally a healthier one. If you don't believe us, just test it out for yourself. The benefits are endless.

Like walking, you can also swim, take a bike ride, go for a gentle jog, do push-ups and sit-ups, jump rope, do gardening, go hiking, even go rollerblading. Other people prefer group exercise, like exercise classes, dance classes, organized team sports, yoga, tai chi—even martial arts classes (though we don't necessarily recommend places that put a focus on aggression and violence). Structured exercise settings such as these can be excellent for assisting in self-discipline, can be very fun, and are also good places to interact with other like-minded people.

Meanwhile, although some people find public exercise places such as this alienating and even humiliating, others find it a good place to make friends. It all depends on your temperament—and how much you can afford!

One thing is for sure: walking is free!

Questions for Self-Reflection

1) How healthy is my lifestyle—and are the lifestyles of those around me?
2) Do I have an adequate support network? If not, how might I be able to improve my support network?
3) Do I spend too much time in isolation?
4) Do I get a good night sleep every night?
5) How healthy is my diet?
6) Do I use drugs and drink alcohol, and if so, how does this affect me?
7) How much effort do I put into practicing healthy exercise?

Chapter 11

Dealing With Money

Common wisdom says that if you want to kill a conversation quickly, start discussing religion or money. Since the details of religion are beyond the scope of this book, let us focus instead on money. Money is often an extremely painful issue for people diagnosed with a psychiatric disorder. A psychiatric disorder commonly goes hand in hand with financial powerlessness. Some people are on SSI or disability, and perhaps Food Stamps or welfare or other sources of government assistance. These are usually barely enough to cover life's basic expenses, if that. This is frustrating, to say the least, and all the more so in a society that so intimately connects a person's worth with his bank account. People look down upon, and even cruelly judge, those who don't "earn their keep" through their own labor.

Other people diagnosed with a psychiatric disorder get financial assistance from their families, which carries its own burden, because, as the saying does, "there is no free lunch." There is always a cost in taking money from people—especially from those who are closest to you. It distorts relationships, and can set up a myriad of resentments. Sometimes families resent having to share their hard-earned money. Other times the person receiving it resents having to take it. It feels like a handout.

It is hard to live as an adult in the world and not work. People stigmatize adults, especially younger adults who are not in school and who don't work, and often treat them as less-than-adult—sometimes even less-than-human. This can be humiliating and frustrating, and make you feel different from others, especially if you want to work but have difficulty finding or holding down a job. And sometimes, to make matters worse, the system of government benefits actually gives you *disincentives* to work: you can lose your monthly check, lose your Food Stamps, even lose your health insurance! That is scary, especially when you consider that going back to work, and dealing with the intense and unknown interactive expectations of the workplace, can be daunting enough on its own.

Some people deal with this by working off the books—at jobs that do not report your income to the government, and which also let you avoid paying taxes. Although this is illegal, it has proven a lifesaver for many. It is a sad comment on our modern world that people who already live confusing, difficult lives are pressured in this direction. Generally off-the-books jobs are not the most prestigious around, but they are work, and do bring in income that can transition people toward a more empowered life.

Other people try volunteer work, which can be more interesting, more flexible, and less pressured than paid work—and sometimes can lead to solid, legal, paid employment. Part-time work can be very helpful too.

Meanwhile, the relationship between a person diagnosed with a psychiatric disorder and his or her family members is often intimately connected with money. When money issues are in turmoil or when money is in short supply—or no supply—the pressure on family relationships can heighten dramatically. Many people who receive a monthly government check go broke before the end of the month, and in those last few days of the monthly poverty cycle often have the most conflicts with their families. You may be desperate at times to borrow money from your relatives, be given gifts from them, or even steal their money. Sometimes this money goes for food, sometimes for necessary travel, sometimes for entertainment or recreation, and sometimes to pay last month's end-of-the-month debts.

We see your goal as taking responsibility for yourself. Taking responsibility is the primary ingredient in maturity. There are many ways to take financial responsibility, but a good goal is to start by creating, and living with, a budget. Others, such as a family member, friend, or therapist, can help you with this, and there are also free support groups, like Debtors Anonymous, which will help guide you. Many people, however, choose to do it on their own.

The key is to write down all the money you bring in, write down all of your expenses—being bluntly honest with yourself—and make sure the two columns add up nicely. The ideal is that you save a little bit of money every month—to give yourself a cushion from whatever potential problems and emergencies might crop up in your future.

People who balance their budgets every month, and live with a little financial cushion, live with much lower levels of anxiety than do people who live in continual financial chaos and debt. And people who live with lower levels of anxiety get along better with their families, and also feel better about themselves as individuals.

No surprise: he who is in control of his money is much more the master of his universe. He owes nothing to anyone, and doesn't have to answer to anyone either. If you stabilize your financial situation, the all-too-common family badgering about money dries right up, like bad fruit on the vine.

But some people feel that it is the responsibility of their families or the government to take care of them financially. They say, "The world wronged *me* and now it owes *me!* *They* have it easy, *they* never went through the hell *I* did. I *deserve* to be taken care of!"

The problem is that the person saying this is not a child. It is only age-appropriate for children to live with this level of entitlement. When adults become so entitled it usually, at the deeper, secret levels, belies a huge amount of fear, sadness, and grief, and the more they stick with this attitude, the lousier they generally feel about themselves. Yes, there may be truth in some of what they say, and we don't wish to take away or deny anyone's history of hell, trauma, and horror, but by the same token, the solution to hell and trauma is to resolve them. Recovery from a psychiatric disorder is rarely helped by wallowing in such thoughts and expecting bailout and rescue from the world. Resolution brings empowerment. Entitlement, on the other hand, is the polar opposite of empowerment.

But perhaps you feel that it is impossible for you to stabilize yourself financially—because you *need* to spend the money you spend, and you simply don't bring in enough money to cover your life's costs. We would reply: maybe you could look more closely at your needs. Many people inflate their financial needs, even to themselves in their private moments. When people have for so long been deprived of so much in their lives, as is true with many people diagnosed with psychiatric disorders, their ability to spend money is one of their last senses of control. The idea of cutting down expenses can feel like torture—like stealing candy from a baby.

In this vein, it is not uncommon for people diagnosed with a psychiatric disorder who have been perpetually in debt to finally go back to work to pay off their debts, only to spend more money than ever—and end up in even more debt!

Out of control spending creates more problems than it solves. We have witnessed that the greater pleasure in life comes from the balance of financial solvency. When people take a cold, hard, dispassionate look at their expenses, and have a serious desire to live within their means, they are able to cut out significant amounts of spending that previously seemed *so necessary* to survival. The reality is that people have lived just fine since time immemorial without cell phones, cable TV, flat-screen televisions, computers, DVD players, video games, high-speed internet access, expensive coffee drinks, surround sound, Coca-Cola, fancy shoes, fancy clothes—even cigarettes! These are not essentials, and often make a person's life worse rather than better. Life's electronic gadgets, which seem to have become life itself in this modern, fast-paced mess of a world, only end up disconnecting us more from our fellows—and keeping us in the house and away from the hustle and bustle of humanity. And we have seen many people on fixed incomes who spend more on cigarettes than on their rent—and would more quickly give up their apartments than their cigarette addictions![39]

We encourage you to prioritize your expenditures. It takes work, flexibility, perseverance, and dedication, but it can be done. And if you can do it, you regain control over your life—and you earn back your self-esteem. And that is priceless.

Questions for Self-Reflection

1) What are my spending habits?
2) Do I know how much money I take in and spend every month?
3) Do I presently live on a reasonable a budget, and if not, can I create one for myself?
4) In what ways am I able to work?
5) What is my financial relationship with my family members like?
6) To what degree, if any, does my financial relationship with my family members cause them or me stress or anxiety?
7) How financially independent am I?
8) What might help me become able to live with more financial independence?

---

[39] In fairness, though, some psychiatric research has shown that cigarette smoking may actually help offset the negative side effects of antipsychotic medication, and can actually stimulate the liver to metabolize the medication more quickly and effectively—which might well explain why so many people diagnosed with schizophrenia are heavy smokers, even when the financial burden on them is excessive. For a compilation of this research, see G. Jackson's book, *Rethinking Psychiatric Drugs: A Guide for Informed Consent*, [(2005). Bloomington, IN: Author House.]

Chapter 12

Getting Help Through Psychotherapy

Psychotherapy has proven to be an invaluable help to many people diagnosed with a major psychiatric disorder, to the degree that some credit it as the primary factor helping them regain their stability in their family, or even recover fully. Other people find psychotherapy a safe and tranquil place to explore their family relationships, their family dynamics, and their family conflicts. At its best this can take massive pressure off the family system, offering you (and, indirectly, your family) a new and more objective perspective on things.

On the other hand, there is no lack of people diagnosed with a major psychiatric disorder who found therapy harmful—for a variety of reasons. Some have felt incredibly misunderstood in therapy, or even judged and shamed. As such, if you are considering entering psychotherapy, it is important that you do so with eyes and mind wide open. Some educated skepticism on your part may prove to be a good quality. For instance, not all therapists are healthy or helpful, despite their degrees and licenses and training. Some have entered the mental health field for odd or controlling reasons of their own. Others have hidden agendas that can prove hurtful to you. Others lack basic knowledge about how to work with people who have more serious emotional problems. And others are very troubled themselves—perhaps even more troubled than the people they are attempting to help. And sometimes there are truly good therapists out there who just may not click with you—or with your needs.

Your job is to trust your intuition, and if you decide to enter therapy, to choose someone with whom *you* feel comfortable. We recognize, however, that not all situations allow you a choice in terms of who you get for a therapist. Many hospitals and clinics simply assign a therapist to you, and it may be very difficult, if not impossible, to switch to someone else if you're not happy.

Sometimes it takes a while to figure out if a therapist is right for you or not. Although it helps if a therapist comes as the result of a recommendation from someone you trust, this is not always possible. Many people find a therapist at a local clinic—or through the yellow pages, the internet, or some other referral service. Others get a referral from a hospital social worker, whom perhaps they've only met once or twice. Regardless, no one would expect you to trust such potential therapists too quickly. After all, you don't even know them—and they don't know you.

As such, you are well within your rights to test them out—to the best of your ability. It is perfectly acceptable for you to ask a potential therapist whatever questions you wish to ask, in spite of what our politeness-oriented society might say. Even personal questions are okay. The key is to see how they respond. Good therapists, like good parents, can handle delicate questions, and they ought to encourage you to ask. Also, they answer in mature, gentle, respectful ways that are helpful to you.

Here are some questions you might ask:

1) How long have you been a therapist?
2) Have you worked with other people with problems similar to mine?
3) What is your opinion on psychiatric medication?
4) Have you ever seen anyone with problems like mine fully recover?
5) Have you ever seen anyone with problems like mine successfully get off medication?
6) What made you want to become a therapist?
7) Do you work on a sliding scale if my health insurance (or present payment source) runs out?
8) What do you like best about being a therapist?
9) What is your opinion on hospitalizing people?
10) Can you relate to me—and to what I am sharing?
11) What do you think is the cause of my problems?
12) What do you think is the solution to my problems?
13) Do you really think I can get well?
14) What do you think will be your role in helping me get well?
15) What is your opinion on my relationship with my family?

Sadly, many people never openly question their therapists—despite the many questions they secretly harbor. We have all wanted to ask our therapists questions, and sometimes we just keep quiet to keep up the polite façade. But holding in questions certainly does not serve the therapy.

Meanwhile, if you do ask questions (the sample ones here—or, better yet, ones of your own) it generally bodes well for the therapy if a therapist responds to them in a way that make you feel more comfortable and safe. Perhaps this will involve the therapist answering some or all of your questions directly, or perhaps not. A good therapist knows that his or her job is to earn your trust, and ultimately to help you to trust the best within yourself. And he or she knows that this takes time.

On the other hand, it is generally a bad sign for the therapy if the therapist's response—or lack of response—makes you feel shamed, uncomfortable, stupid, or self-hating. This generally signals that they don't know what they're doing, and will not prove to be that useful for you in the long run. How, after all, can you expect to explore your life and your most intimate relationships and your most personal feelings if your therapist shames or belittles your questions at the very beginning of the relationship?

Yet sadly, this is all too common. But should we be surprised? The standards of the modern mental health system are that many therapists have little or no real experience (much less training) helping people diagnosed with a major psychiatric disorder. Most are trained to work with people with milder problems—and many therapists don't even do that too effectively. And most psychiatrists, who occupy the top rung of the mental health field, have little or no experience doing real psychotherapy with anyone!

In this vein, many, if not most, therapists have never seen someone recover from a major psychiatric disorder, and thus don't even consider this a realistic possibility. These are therapists worth avoiding. After all, would you feel comfortable going to a cancer doctor who had no experience helping anyone recover from cancer, a business consultant who had never helped a client turn a profit, or a roofer who had never properly repaired a roof?

Sometimes a major psychiatric disorder scares therapists—and even threatens them. It is all too easy to label things that frighten us as "delusions" and "hallucinations" and to hide behind pathologizing diagnostic words like "mania" and "thought disorder" and "borderline personality" and "schizophrenia."[40] Other therapists feel incompetent or insecure because more severe problems are out of their range of experience or beyond their expertise. That is why so many therapists, when dealing with people diagnosed with a major psychiatric disorder, think only medication or hospitalization is helpful. They truly don't know any better.

Some therapists don't even know where to start in terms of being really useful to you. They have difficulty listening to your problems and concerns, and being really empathic. As such, you are well within your rights to ask as many probing questions as you want about what kind of experience your therapist has in working with people with problems like yours. Your job, after all, is to honor *your* feelings and honor *your* healing path, and do what is in *your own best interest*. And each person's best interest is different. As such, finding a flexible therapist who doesn't believe in a one-size-fits-all approach is usually best. To use an analogy, if you drove a Volkswagen and needed it repaired, would you take it to a mechanic who only repaired Chevrolets?

Meanwhile, your family might prefer a different therapist for you. Perhaps they have an alternate idea of what you need. Although it might be good to consider their ideas, ultimately it is you who are the client or consumer, you who are seeking the help, and you who sit with the therapist and develop a relationship with him or her. So ultimately the choice is yours.

Also, you are well within your rights to interview several therapists and keep moving on until you find one that works. This is part of being an informed consumer—and any good therapist will understand and respect this. Some will even encourage it!

Sometimes the quest to find a good therapist takes many tries. Some people try out five or more therapists before they settle on one that feels most beneficial. This process can be uncomfortable and guilt-producing, especially if you are someone who was raised to make others happy at your own expense. But good therapists *are* out there and *are* available—if you seek. If you are lucky—and persevere—you will find such a person.

---

[40] Hebert Strean, a prominent therapist, refers to this as "diagnostic name-calling." [See, H. Strean and L. Freeman (1988). *Behind the Couch: Revelations of a Psychoanalyst.* John Wiley and Sons.]

Questions for Self-Reflection

1) What is my experience with psychotherapy?
2) Have I ever had a therapist who was very helpful to me?
3) What fears, if any, do I have about psychotherapy?
4) If I am in therapy, am I satisfied with my therapist?
5) Are there questions I would secretly like to ask my therapist but am afraid to ask?
6) What is stopping me from asking these questions?
7) Might I like to try a different therapist?
8) What are the qualities I would best like in a potential therapist?
9) What might I like to gain from psychotherapy?

Chapter 13

Distance Versus Closeness with Your Family

Everyone develops the relationship with his or her family that works best for him or her. So many factors go into this, including the degree of supportiveness and respect that you receive from your parents and siblings, your own temperament and needs, your degree of shared common perspective, your anger at them and perhaps theirs at you, the degree of love and comfort you feel while interacting with them, and perhaps, most simply, how nice they are to you—and how nice you are to them.

Different degrees of closeness versus distance with your family can all be appropriate. Some people find a balanced family relationship that involves a lot of shared time, shared events, shared meals, shared holidays, and sometimes even shared living situations. Other people discover that a balanced family relationship involves significant distance. Sometimes this means living in a different geographical location, getting an unlisted phone number, perhaps not even seeing or talking with your parents or siblings for months or years at a time. While this can be painful for all involved, sometimes in the long run it can actually be quite helpful—and reset old, unhealthy patterns and troubled boundaries that no amount of discussion or even family therapy could have helped. And sometimes, when reconnections happen after a period of distance, relationships improve dramatically—to everyone's surprise.[41]

Family relationships can be so painful, but they can also be so nourishing. Your job is to find the balance that works best for you, that best assists you on your life's path and your recovery. Your job is to maximize the quality of your relationships, and minimize the

---

[41] This is a common theme in many, if not most, of the contributors' chapters at the end of this volume.

unnecessary conflict and turmoil. Your job is to get well, whatever "well" might mean to you.

Many times your family has a different conception from yours of what they would like in their relationship with you—and what they would like to see in your life. Although your job is to respect them, your bigger job is to respect yourself—and find what truly works for you. Honoring yourself in this way is key to your recovery. In this vein, their job is to respect you, and also to find out what works for them. If both you and they honor your own selves, there is almost always enough overlap for some sort of positive relationship. But sometimes this takes time, and sometimes a long time. Finding a compromise takes work—sometimes years of hard work.

Some people go through periods of confronting their parents. This is risky, because confrontations generally do not produce "loving" or "supportive" results. Confrontations generally create a lot of stress and sometimes even chaos—and hospitalization. But in certain situations, confrontations, if handled well, can bring certain issues to light, and can even provoke resolution.

We, however, do not encourage you to confront your parents about anything until you have first expended a major amount of effort into stabilizing your life, building yourself a strong base of support outside the family, and developing a powerfully healthy lifestyle. Otherwise, you risk disintegrating your life, and putting yourself at the mercy of a world that might not be so supportive, and might even be quite destructive. Also, if you are going to confront your parents it is better that you do so when *you are not living with them.* This gives both you and them healthy distance, and takes much of the pressure off the confrontation.

Additionally, in some cases we recommend that confrontations be balanced with appreciations, for instance, making effort to note some of the good things that your parents are doing or may have done. Confrontations that are direct attacks tend to produce far worse results than those that are more balanced.

Meanwhile, if you take responsibility for yourself as an adult, learn about your historical and present role in the family, work to develop a greater sense of self-respect, build stronger boundaries in your relationships, learn to nurture your own emotional healing process through grieving every ounce of your losses, and develop a healthier overall lifestyle, your relationships with your family will improve. This may not be readily apparent at first, because sometimes change, no matter how positive, can feel negative for a time. But in the end, healthiness only leads to more healthiness.

If you become healthier in your life, perhaps it will make your family uncomfortable. This has happened in many cases. It will throw off the ancient balance that was not working, and will pressure them, even force them, to readjust, and they may not like this at first. This is more common than one would expect. But if they are truly on your side, they will readjust, and accept the new you.

Likewise, if they become healthier than you more rapidly than you are becoming healthy, and they practice "tough love" with you in ways that make it difficult for you to keep practicing certain unhealthy patterns, you will probably react negatively to them—at first. But if you are committed to growing healthier and stronger, and you look deep within yourself and assess the appropriateness of what they are doing, you will accept their changes, even if it hurts for a while.

If only change were painless! If only growth were easy! If only converting unhealthy patterns into healthy ones were simple and straightforward!

Alas, life is a complex process and can often be difficult and frustrating and painful, but if we stay on course, focus on what we need to do each day, every day, we cannot help but grow—and find hope. And our family relationships will inevitably reflect that.

Questions for Self-Reflection

1) What type of balance would I like to achieve with my family?
2) Am I ready to live on my own?
3) Do I like my relationship with my family?
4) What things do I still need to do to improve my relationship with my family members?
5) Do I wish to confront my family members?
6) Have my confrontations been appropriate or inappropriate?
7) Have my confrontations been helpful to me?

Section II

Contributors' Chapters

Chapter 14

Points of No Return—Turning Points with Family

by Annie G. Rogers (with Mary M. Rogers)

> Editors' Introduction: *Annie Rogers, Ph.D. is a professor of psychoanalysis and clinical psychology at Hampshire College in Massachusetts, and prior to that was a professor and researcher at Harvard University. She is the author of two books,* A Shining Affliction *and* The Unsayable: The Hidden Language of Trauma, *and the editor of two more. She is also a watercolor painter and published poet. She co-wrote the following chapter with her sister, Mary M. Rogers—her strongest ally in her recovery from schizophrenia.*

I knew from childhood that I was different in some way that I could not define for myself, and I did not speak about my strange experiences. But by the time I was an adolescent, I was living in a waking dream much of the time, a dream that went on and on, with no point of return. I was hearing voices coming from unexpected places: a book cabinet, the radiator, the trees...and continually working to "translate" them. These voices spoke in code; I created an alphabet and a language to translate this "celestial language," a language that would make it possible for humans to speak to one another and stop destroying each other. I was a modern-day Joan of Arc, put to work by those voices. But the Catholic Church, particularly the bishops and archbishops, kept trying to intervene, and they could set splinters embedded in my arms alight, and burn me alive. To me, this reality was irrefutable, and it was far removed from any concerns with my family. My peers and family thought I was taking drugs, but I was not. After a suicide attempt at age sixteen, I was hospitalized in a private psychiatric hospital. During that time, I was initially diagnosed as manic-depressive and given electric shock therapy, which changed nothing. Seven months later and still in the hospital at seventeen, I was diagnosed as schizophrenic.

As a child in the early years of grade school, I did not become friends with my schoolmates. I barely knew their names. But my sister Mary, less than a year older than I, played with me, and she pulled me into a playing group in the neighborhood. She oriented me to the world around us and she was fiercely protective of me. I loved reading and language as a child, as she did. We made up roles and scripts and played them out with stuffed animals. At age eleven, I began a continuous set of journals, and wrote little plays and poems. In high school, after I'd attempted suicide twice, I remember as I was falling asleep one night in the bedroom that I shared with Mary, she said, "If you succeed in killing yourself, I'm going to publish your journals." I did not answer. Was this a threat, or was it a promise? If it was a threat, then she wanted me to live, and if it was a promise, then she believed in me as a writer. As it turned out, it was both.

My mother's eyes were deep as puddles after a rain. Always a "lady," she arched her eyebrows when she was pleased, and smiled with her lips closed. My mother descended every stairway slowly, even when we were in a hurry. She tapped the back of each step with her heel, as though she were not sure the stairs were really there. She had been in a fire as a young woman, and she was lucky to have lived. She was also an active alcoholic before I was born. In fact, my parents met in AA. Yet I cannot imagine her drinking, or drunk. As she squinted at the stairs through her bifocals, I wondered if her way of taking the stairs developed during those years when her world tilted?

When my sister and I were five and six years old, our father died and our mother lived with us in a small apartment. During these years, I do not know what she suffered. She imposed a regular physical torment on me when we were alone, and I will not speak of that here—there is simply no room to do so. Most of the time, she stayed inside and did not interact much with people beyond us. We came and went, going to school (somewhat irregularly), out to play, running errands. When I was ten and my sister eleven, we were placed in a Children's Home for four years, because a court decided that my mother was not able to care for us. When we returned to our mother, she made a huge effort to learn to be in the world for us. She joined the Church, made friends, and worked at the City Courts giving directions and information to the public. She sent us to the best parochial high school in the city on scholarships. She bought us bicycles, took in a cat (who became the family pet), and when I was hospitalized, she negotiated with the administration of St. Vincent's Hospital to keep me in a private psychiatric hospital.

When I was diagnosed schizophrenic and the hospital would no longer keep me, the psychiatrist in charge of my case told my mother that I would have to go to the State Hospital for an indefinite time. I do not know what she said to make it otherwise. I only know that I came home then, and that my mother spoke with my school, and I was readmitted. I'd missed most of my junior year of high school, and when I returned I was not able to draw in perspective, and not able to study very well. I remember my mother taking me with her to work and sitting on the floor behind her desk, just terrified. But, for the most part, I went to school again. After that awful spring and summer, as I entered my senior year, a space of lucidity opened up for me. I did two years of school work in a year, wrote and produced a play in my final semester, and graduated from high school with my class.

I knew that my mother had literally given me a chance at life again, but I could not tell her anything of my experience. In fact, we were not at all close. At the time I barely understood the enormity of what she'd done. I learned later that my father had committed suicide in that state hospital, and that my half-brother (autistic and severely retarded) had been a patient there for several years. When my mother was dying of cancer and I was in my early thirties, for the first time it was possible to speak to her, as if death coming so swiftly had stripped away all but the most crucial things, making it possible to hear her, and to be heard. I understood then that she had her own suffering, her own struggles, a life before me, and would meet her death without me—she was beyond me, and yet I was of her, her child, a child she loved enough to keep out of the state hospital.

Throughout my late adolescence and all through my twenties, I was in and out of mental hospitals. I was given Haldol and Cogentin, and sometimes sleeping medication. I did not take these medicines once I was out of the hospital. They did no good, and only made me feel that I barely existed. The side effects of pacing and back spasms were truly awful. I wanted to be a writer, and except during periods when I was too confused to navigate the world, I went to school and studied through my hallucinations. I lived at home after a semester away at college (followed by another crisis and hospitalization), and completed college in five and a half years, summa cum laude. I began graduate school in literature, and then switched to psychology.

As a young adult I sought out and paid to see a psychologist during my college years, and this work gave me a foothold in navigating the social world without my sister. I applied for disability funds to support my fees and hoped to live apart from my family. I was appalled at the assumptions of the caseworker assigned to me, who could not believe I was doing so well in school and predicted a dire future, especially once he learned that I refused medication. I did not believe him, and also refused the offer of funding, opting to walk away, continue to live at home, and work for the money I needed for my therapy. I also remember going to an outpatient clinic and a young doctor explaining to me just why I had to stay on my medications. I found him compelling, but did not follow his advice.

While I was in graduate school I was hospitalized two to three times each year, usually for a couple of weeks at a time. In my late twenties, following the worst crisis I experienced in which the voices I heard were telling me to commit murder and then suicide, I entered a time of such chaos that it is difficult to say what happened. This time my mother was not involved, and it was Mary who intervened, speaking to me directly. Though I do not recall the conversation, I know that it was a turning point, from a point that seemed to have no return. Her story is part of my story since childhood. She has agreed to write about this small part of it here.

***

Annie and I have always been close sisters. We are the only children of our parents' marriage, less than a year apart in age. In early childhood and especially after our father died and our mother withdrew from the world, we were virtually inseparable. The close bond we shared as young children waned in adolescence. This distance was accentuated by the closeness of the relationship that I had forged with our mother beginning early in high school. At the same time Annie's relationship with our mother seemed at its most strained. Sometime in early adulthood, Annie and I both set out to establish our independent lives, with apartments out of the neighborhood we grew up in. This was difficult for our mother. Her health was beginning to deteriorate and her network of friends was shrinking. I think that of all the things she thought might be part of her older years, our mother never envisioned what it would be like for her children to grow up to have their own lives apart from hers. Annie and I found ourselves reaching out to each other and finding in the other an old and true friend. We were frequent visitors to each other's apartments; we cooked meals together, took walks together.

The last time that Annie was hospitalized was also the only time that our mother did not play a role in her hospitalization. Instead, as Annie descended once again into the nightmare of psychosis (I realize that I don't even have the words to describe that nightmare), she reached out to a close circle of friends and to me. She pleaded with me not to tell our mother. So it fell to me, Annie's sister, to try to be her advocate in a system I didn't fully understand, while she was fighting a disease I couldn't comprehend.

As it turned out, neither did the professionals treating her. As Annie fell deeper and deeper into psychosis, all of her familiar little expressions, her gestures and finally even her language disappeared. The person I visited in the hospital looked like my sister and wore her clothes, but the resemblance ended there. This Annie spoke a kind of "word salad," that is, she used words in the English language, but in no recognizable grammar or grouping of words that conveyed meaning. I had seen Annie hospitalized many other times and I had grown used to the effects that medication and electroconvulsive therapy had on her, but this was different.

I tried to explain this to her doctor and to my surprise, found him asking me if I thought I could detect any changes in Annie as he increased, reduced, and changed her medications. I remember at one point, I suggested that he decrease her medication and he did. I was guessing wildly, but it seemed that every time her medication was increased, the Annie that I knew was there less and less. It was a truly terrifying time.

The height of terror for me came when the hospital social worker told me that Annie's health insurance would no longer support her stay and that we would need to plan for her transfer to the state hospital. This just couldn't happen. As I had promised not to involve our mother, I couldn't use her experience to help us either.

So I did the only other thing I could think of. When I visited with Annie, even though it didn't appear that she could understand anything I said to her, I had to try and reach her. We sat in her room.

She lay on her bed, facing the wall. What followed is a conversation I will always remember. I explained, "Annie, I don't think you can understand me, but I have to try and help you understand. You have to come back to yourself. If you can't, they are going to send you to the state hospital and I can't stop them from doing it. You need to come back here and you need to do it soon. Do you understand?" There was, as I had feared, no response.

But on my visit the next day, I thought I detected a glimmer of something familiar in Annie's mannerisms. It was very slight; I don't remember even what it was, and at the time, I was pretty sure I was imagining it. But over the next few days, Annie slowly came back to us. She was still in very bad shape; she couldn't go home. One of Annie's teachers from college invited her to stay with his family. Her doctor agreed. She was enough herself to be able to leave the hospital and begin the long road to recovery.

We have talked about that time in Annie's life many times. I can never explain to either of our satisfaction how, despite all outward appearances, and her own lack of recollection, my words somehow seemed to reach the deepest and most intact part of her.

***

When I began to write this chapter, Mary and I spoke about this "last" crisis, and I still do not recall her speaking to me. In fact, I did not take in that she, like my mother, did something to keep me from going into an institution where I might have stayed indefinitely. It is uncanny to see this repetition, and to feel my life returned to me, not once, but twice. I can envision my sister, her fear and her courage as she spoke to me, though I have no memory of this. I know that she carried her worry and her love alone.

Following this crisis, I began to work with a psychoanalyst and, after four years, I was free of all symptoms and not taking any medications. I finished my Ph.D. in psychology and moved to Cambridge, Massachusetts, where I was a post-doctoral fellow at Harvard for five years, and then a member of the faculty for ten years. I have done clinical work with children and adolescents for twenty years now and currently teach at Hampshire College, in Amherst, Massachusetts. I have also been a part of seminars offered by the Freudian School of Quebec in Canada for the past eight years. This school has pioneered a successful treatment of young psychotic adults through psychoanalysis. I hope to find a way to make some contribution to this school, though I don't yet know what that is.

I have a wonderful partner, Ide B. O'Carroll, the love of my life, and we are married in Massachusetts. I live with her in America, but also for part of the year in Ireland, where we have a home in a small rural town. We have been living together, navigating a life across the Atlantic, for fourteen years.

Looking back on my late adolescence and early adulthood, I can see now that I made crucial choices that, together with my family's interventions, made coming back from a place of no return possible. First of all, I resisted becoming identified with a mental illness. I had wanted to be a writer before my first hospitalization, and that remained a primary sense of what I would do, who I would become. My experience in watching others receive a diagnosis of major mental illness at a young age is that such an identity can become a life path. It need not.

When I was beginning to work as a psychologist, I remember my mother looking at me and saying, "What? They are going to let *you* see patients?!" And I knew that I was taking a risk in forging a space to meet the suffering of children and adolescents as a clinician. Perhaps there is something you, too, wish to do or become, and you must come up against your own or others' disbelief and risk your own belief in yourself.

Finally, the decision to take on paying for my own therapy, and particularly to find a psychoanalyst, to work with him for years, and to pay for that treatment myself, were crucial choices in opening up a life for me that would have otherwise been impossible. I did not have money or come from a family with money. It was my responsibility to choose to live in the world, to choose lucidity—beyond thinking about genetics, or chemistry, or family, or fault, or anything at all—except that I wanted to live.

There are traces of my experience that remain with me, a part of who I am. I have lost years of my life that I can't have back. I look younger than I am as a result of this, I think. I find it difficult to meet and speak to new people. Yet, for all of that, I teach young people and love teaching them. I have found a way to speak through writing poetry, memoir, and fiction—my life as a writer remains vital. What I am trying to say here is simply this—you can make a place for yourself in the world apart from your diagnosis and follow that path until it becomes your life. You can have a place in humanity, and be a part of something bigger than you or I could do alone.

As for your family, what can I possibly say to you? You have lived with them and know each person in your family as I do not. They are the crucible that formed you, your cradle and your legacy, if also at times, your torment. And yet their lives are not your life. You have this one life and its possibilities. Perhaps they can accompany you in your life—with all their frailties and strengths.

Chapter 15

"If Our David Wants to Try Freedom...": Families as Allies and Allies as Family

by David Oaks

> *Editors' Introduction: David Oaks is a world-renowned psychiatric survivor and social justice advocate. He is the executive director of MindFreedom International, which unites thousands of members internationally through a coalition of over one hundred grassroots organizations. He co-founded MindFreedom in 1986 to advocate for human rights and alternatives in the mental health system. David was diagnosed with schizophrenia and manic-depression while an undergraduate at Harvard, though he has recovered completely. He presently lives with his wife, Debra, in Oregon.*

The last time I was locked up in a psychiatric institution—and I hope it proves to be the very last time—the mental health authorities wanted to keep me a lot longer, but my family stood up for me. This happened more than three decades ago. I was a twenty-one year old who had grown up in a working class neighborhood on the south side of Chicago, and I was in my senior year at Harvard on a variety of scholarships, including one from my father's union. From my clothing style to my rough sense of humor, I really did not fit in well at the more upper class-oriented Harvard.

This was the fifth time in three years—as a sophomore, junior and senior—that I had ended up in a psychiatric institution, with stays ranging from a few days to a few weeks, and with diagnoses such as "schizophrenia," "depression" and what would later be called "bipolar."

In the beginning of my senior year, a Harvard social service agency had placed me as a volunteer in a social change group led by survivors of psychiatric abuse, sometimes affectionately known as the "mad movement." So when I ended up in a psychiatric institution for this fifth, and hopefully last, time, members of the Mental Patients Liberation Front (MPLF) were there to help. They visited me, and supported my human rights during my stay in the famous McLean Hospital, a Harvard teaching hospital often voted one of the best in the world.

I did not find my stays in McLean very helpful. In fact, I found the whole experience extremely traumatic, what with the labeling, the forced psychiatric drug injections I endured while being held down on a bare mattress in a solitary confinement room cell, and—worst of all—the hopelessness engendered by being told, falsely, that I had a genetically-caused biochemical imbalance that would require a lifetime of powerful psychiatric drugs. I especially found the neuroleptic drugs to be torture, both because of the physical effects they caused, such as involuntary muscle movement, and also because they were a kind of wrecking ball to the cathedral of my mind.

Somehow, during that final stay in McLean, heavily drugged, I managed to listen on the phone as an MPLF member carefully and slowly explained how to write and file a letter asking to be released against medical advice. I laboriously copied down the letter, signed it, and handed it in. The authorities would have three days to either let me out, or go to court.

I found out later that the psychiatric authorities wanted to hold me, and contacted my family and asked to seek a court order to hold me in McLean. But by this point my family, having listened to me describe the abuse I was going through—and having seen me re-hospitalized several times—was skeptical of the mental health professionals, and my mother famously replied on behalf of our family, "If our David wants to try freedom, we'll support him." My mother later explained to me that she knew there were serious risks, such as suicide, of giving an extremely distressed young man his freedom. But my parents felt that the psychiatric professionals did not really know the "real David." And she was right.

Thankfully, after getting free of the psychiatric system, I used a variety of alternatives for my own mental and emotional well-being, including nutrition, exercise, mutual support, wilderness outings, and family support. My family's support was key. In fact, my brother quit his job in Chicago and drove out to Massachusetts to make sure that I, his kid brother, fifteen months younger, managed to finish up at Harvard. I ended up graduating with honors in 1977 and I've stayed out of the psychiatric system ever since.

Yet what led my family at that critical moment to agree to let me "try freedom?" And what helped me love freedom enough to try? I can guess at a lot of factors.

First, my family and I have a deep appreciation for freedom. This is not just personal, but perhaps part of our cultural heritage. All of my grandparents emigrated from Lithuania, a country that is at the crossroads of turbulent European history and is known for its own brand of rebelliousness and love of liberty. While I speak only a few words of Lithuanian, when I was going through my emotional crises I somehow felt that this ancient language and culture, experienced through my family, affirmed a life of the mind and relationships in a far richer and more complex way than the simple robotic conventions—eat, sleep, work, buy—that make up what is known as "normality."

Second, my family has a history of social activism that was not openly discussed while I was growing up. To this day, I'm sure that most of my relatives would minimize this part of our history, but to me it has significance. My grandfathers both worked significant stints as coal miners in rural Illinois before they moved to Chicago. To this day I have one of my grandfather's union cards (and my father's) on my wall. While I have no evidence either was involved in labor organizing, I do know a bit of the rugged history about the time and place where each worked, including the horrendous Cherry Coal Mine disaster and the mass shooting of workers considered scabs in what is now called the Herrin Massacre.

In this vein, I've recently found out that a few of my other relatives were openly involved in social justice movements decades ago. For example, at the start of the Great Depression my grandmother helped carry a banner in a Communist march against hunger, taking along my then-twelve year old mother. Also, I've discovered I had a great uncle who was passionate about socialism. And a few other relatives were negatively impacted by the anti-Communist Red Scare of the 1950s. It seems that activism was lurking in my blood—certainly more than chemical imbalances were!

Paradoxically, one of my great strengths, the esteem and pride I derived from my family and ethnic culture of rebelliousness and activism, may also have created a vulnerability in me that contributed to my breakdown. Like many in my "boomer" generation, I rebelled by smoking too much cannabis and this over-use played a role in derailing and disempowering me as a young person. While my substance abuse was a clear sign of my internal distress, it is more difficult to understand "why" I was abusing the marijuana and what could have prevented it. Certainly, like many people awakened by the social change movements at the time, I intuitively recognized that an enormous sickness lay at the heart of our society. I did not feel that I could reconcile myself to such a society, and felt apart from it. At the same time, I also sensed that there was something far deeper to what we perceive as reality than the mundane surface normality we come to accept. I craved access to the altered states of mind that mystics had described. Perhaps my intense alienation could have been addressed by closer relationships with and guidance by mentors and peers. However, I found mainly isolation, except when it came to participating in substance abuse with a few people my own age.

Conflicts with My Family

When I developed what would be considered a psychiatric disorder, this led to some of my greatest conflicts with my family. In my altered states, which lasted for years, I experienced many classic signs of what is labeled psychosis, such as believing a neighbor whom I thought was with the CIA was making my teeth grow, that the television was speaking only to me, that I was experiencing the bomb of Hiroshima in my shower, that the sports section of the newspaper was talking about me in code, and more. I do not believe such altered states automatically result in violence. However, when conflict arose, it manifested itself in unique ways that could be distressing for my family.

For example, I remember one New Year's Eve when my parents, concerned about my mental crises, refused to let me out of the house to party with friends. In a dream-like state, I became convinced that the tip of a rock that I had in my bedroom needed—for cosmic reasons—to be pressed very hard against my storm window. In other words, I broke a window. Meanwhile, I knew my family was seeking psychiatric institutionalization for me, and I recall the experience of pleading that this quest be called off. At one point there was a delay in placing me in a Chicago psychiatric facility because the beds were filled. As we waited at home for those few days, I felt calmer, and therefore sought to head off my lock-up. However, since the course of action was already set, my parents—perhaps not wanting to upset the psychiatric apple cart—continued forward. I remember the futility and frustration of trying to argue for my freedom as I was inevitably locked up one more time.

I know now they were desperate, unsure of where to turn or what to do. However, when they took steps to enter me into a psychiatric institution, I felt deeply betrayed.

But thankfully their betrayal was not permanent. My family was flexible, and open to learning and change, and this was to my benefit. Instead of rigidly siding with the mental health "authorities," they dug deeper to find ways to support and understand me. For instance, one time when I was home in Chicago I remember my live-in Uncle Al trying to support me in his own way. I told him that I literally felt a wall was caving in on me. Uncle Al, who had an interest in the paranormal, said he would hold up the wall, and he moved his chair against the wall. This non-professional intuitive affirmation of the dignity of my extreme despair was helpful.

My parents, I feel, also went through a sort of transformation themselves. They were children of the Depression and World War II, a generation sometimes called the "silent majority." One of my father's favorite pieces of advice about life, words that he repeated to me many times, was "David, never ever get angry." The only time I recall our family really "bucking the system" is when a stylish pair of my shoes from Sears developed a hole rather quickly. When at first the clerk would not give a replacement, our family stood its ground. We won. This level of ferment was so infrequent that the memory of the Great Shoe Rebellion stays with me.

So when their precious son was in crisis, at first my parents clung to the perspective of the medical authorities as a kind of gospel. I wonder if they began to doubt the doctors the time they visited me in my hospital bed, and I developed severe muscular paroxysms throughout my body, requiring an emergency injection of a muscle relaxant. I'm not saying my parents became vocal critics of the mental health system, but they did become just skeptical enough to refuse to seek a court order on me during that crucial moment of my last institutionalization. If they had sought a court order, I think my spirit could have been broken, and I might still be on neuroleptics today, after three decades, which I believe would have permanently damaged my mind.

In some ways then, my emotional crises as a young adult helped deepen my connection to my family. It helped bring out some of their best qualities in relation to me—their caring and compassion and struggle on my behalf. On the other hand, I've always felt a certain barrier in my extended family because of society's prejudice against psychiatric diagnosis, what may be called "sanism," a discrimination that is so deep it is seldom named. At family gatherings I still sense that some of my relatives have a discomfort and vagueness about my past and my work. With the advent of the Internet, though, some of them have been able to read my brief biography—and better understand my mental health history and my chosen occupation. In fact, now a number of relatives tell me they are fans of my work, and cheer it on.

That said, I suppose part of the way I dealt with family issues was a kind of self-imposed exile from family. Or perhaps, more accurately, I made a transition from mainly relying on my biological family to also relying on an extended family of activists who would not be considered relatives. I moved to Oregon, where I now live and work, and most of my family resides in Illinois and Texas. I've made social change in mental health my career, and I direct MindFreedom International. I stay on good terms with my biological family and to this day, my mom, who is now in her nineties, is one of our main volunteers, doing quality office work.

A Look Toward the Future

If I were to advise young people in their early twenties who, like me, find themselves surrounded by the mental health system, I'd recommend that they pay special attention to maintaining their own independence, including economic independence. In other words, one of the best skills you may need in navigating your family, and navigating the larger world beyond your family, would be job skills.

Here, interestingly enough, I credit my mother. Although I studied community organizing which proved invaluable to me in the long-term, on a more direct level I was helped by my mother. Although both my parents highly valued education, they also valued practical work skills, as this was the world they knew. One of the things that helped me get free of the mental health system after college was something my mother taught me as a pre-teen, years before I entered the psychiatric system: office skills. With encouragement from my father, she taught me to type on those old manual typewriters. At the age of fifteen I obtained a special work permit to become an office clerk at her job in downtown Chicago. This meant that when I graduated from Harvard, I had immediately useable job skills. I worked dozens of temporary office positions all over the country. Having an independent source of income meant that I could develop my own sense of independence, which was incredibly psychologically liberating.

Moving from practical to psychological advice, I'd also advise this: "I encourage you to realize you play a role in helping the rest of the family during your very own crisis. That is, every one of your family members who cares about you can become upset during your crisis. Perhaps they themselves do not have the experience, skills and knowledge to deal with this distress. Some may need comfort and reassurance. Occasionally, some you will need to avoid."

Thankfully, in my situation, my family was unified on my behalf, and no family member became an opponent to my freedom. However, since then I have talked to countless young adults who faced crises similar to mine, yet their family unit was split. Perhaps their father was for forced psychiatric drugging while their mother opposed it. I do not have an easy answer for such a tragedy. If my family had strongly divided against itself over my fate in the mental health system, I think my only recourse would have been to secretly escape from the opponent family member as far away as possible without any contact, until my freedom was secure.

Finally and most importantly, while family support is important, the support of a network of peers is equally important. When I filed what was called a "three day letter" to apply to get out of my hopefully last psychiatric institution, my biological family supported me. However, it was a kind of new, intentional, non-biological family composed of activists in our social change movement who supplied me with the self-determination and empowerment to stand up for my basic human rights, and to sustain my freedom for the long haul. This small ragtag band of psychiatric survivors became my new family, and taught me about better diet, exercise, nature outings, mutual support and even the role of protest in true recovery. Community organizing is similar to intentionally building a chosen family of supportive people. Our society segregates biological from non-biological family. However, ultimately, we are all "cousins" on this planet. Our "family" includes the family of humanity.

I would ask not only people with psychiatric labels but all people a question: "What community of supportive people—what family, both biological and metaphorical—are you joining, and helping to build around you?"

Chapter 16

The Harm of Early Hurt

by Carol Hebald

> Editors' Introduction: *Carol Hebald, MFA is an award-winning poet and writer in New York City. For many years she was a professor of writing at various universities around the country, and prior to that a successful actress on and off Broadway. Her books include the novella collection* Three Blind Mice, *the poetry collection* Spinster by the Sea, *and her memoir* The Heart Too Long Suppressed: A Chronicle of Mental Illness. *Diagnosed with schizophrenia for years, she is completely recovered and has been out of the mental health system for nearly thirty years.*

My Early Years

I was three years old when my father, an Austrian immigrant of fifty-five, began to feel a little tired and had lost his too-hearty appetite. A New York Bowery jeweler, he worked twelve-hour shifts, from ten in the morning till ten at night, seven days a week. When his complexion began to yellow, the doctor took one look at him and knew: he had liver cancer. He stopped working and rested at home while my mother took charge of his store.

He'd call me often to his room. I'd creep into his bed where he read me his favorite passages from Shakespeare's plays. We spent his last year together. When his nurse knocked on the door, he'd yell, "Stay out, I'm with my daughter."

One afternoon I caught sight of him masturbating in his pajamas.

"Come a little closer," he said. He told me to undress and I obeyed.

Later, recalling our sexual contact, I was never able to muster the "appropriate rage" I'm supposed to have felt. I find it impossible to hate the man whose agonized screams still echo in my ear.

Eventually, he grew too ill to see me. He died in 1938 when I was four.

In keeping with the custom of the day the fact was withheld from me. When I asked Mother, "Where's Daddy?" she told me, "Daddy went far away on a long, long trip."

I waited every day.

Our last words remain in my memory: "Daddy, what should I be when I grow up?"

"Be somebody."

"*Who?*"

My mother, a Junoesque beauty of thirty-seven, dressed every morning for the store, where she continued to work my father's grueling hours. I'd follow her from room to room.

"That child is always following me around," she complained. "That child is always asking questions."

I began to lose my thoughts. I'd have something vitally important to say. No sooner would I open my mouth than I'd forget it.

"What is it you want?" she screamed.

I wanted to tell her that every morning after she left, our Hungarian maid Barbara would lock me in a dark closet all day. Why, I didn't know. But Barbara threatened to kill me if I told.

Did I bang to get out? I don't remember. My entrance into fantasy was swift. A sleeve became my father's hand, a silk dress my mother's breast, a fur coat my father's chest... Barbara would let me out just before my big sister Jani came home from school, so I assume my mother didn't know—until I told her several years later when Barbara had temporarily returned to her native Hungary with the object of finding a husband. When she came back triumphant my mother rehired her.

I asked Mother whether she'd forgotten what Barbara had done to me.

"Of course not! But you're a big girl now," she cajoled. "And don't you agree that Barbara cooks the best chicken *paprikás* you ever tasted?"

I was eight when I stopped trusting my mother.

I began sneaking out of the house to go to the nearby Loews

Delancey movie theater. Money in hand, I'd ask a lady on line to take me in. Then I'd sit alone in the Children's Section. The first time a gentleman joined me and, hat in lap, exposed himself my nerves flooded with familiar pleasure. This had happened somewhere before. It would happen again and again. I didn't remember my father's sexual abuse until years later in a psychiatrist's office.

I never understood what was happening on the movie screen. The noise of words disturbed me. Nor could I listen in school, where I'd sass my teacher in frustration. She'd stand me in the corner with a dunce cap on or shove me into the wastebasket under her desk. I couldn't read until I was nine. So poor was my concentration, I was put in a slow learners' class. In danger of being left back, I begged my sister to teach me to read. And good Jani *did* teach me, that spring in Central Park.

I was eleven when my mother remarried, and after eight years behind the counter finally sold the jewelry store. The upheaval of circumstances upset me deeply. A half-orphan, I wanted to be a whole one, to start life over—but not with these parents.

That spring, I walked out of a film and had what I thought was a revelation from God. I heard no astral melody; no angel descended on a cloud. Just an unearthly voice echoing in a radiance of light: "You will be a great actress."

I went immediately to the Drama Bookshop and bought Stanislavski's *An Actor Prepares*. I learned that acting is an art, and experience the artist's hunting ground. For us, suffering is neither random nor meaningless so long as we can put it to use. For me, the harm of early hurt now had a purpose. No longer was I a discipline problem at school. I barely spoke; I did my work.

I was a sophomore Drama Major at the High School of Performing Arts when the department head told me I had the power to thrill an audience, but she felt strongly that I needed psychological help. She referred me to the outpatient division of the Payne Whitney clinic, where my history as a mental patient began.

Early Adulthood

I went straight from High School into the commercial theater. By age twenty-five, the proud veteran of two Broadway shows, I'd fulfilled my father's dying wish that I *be somebody*. On good days, I entered the playwright's personae, and was praised for the authentic suffering with which I endowed them. But my days were not all good.

Whipsawed between a hunger to succeed and a need to be nurtured, I was sadly lacking in actor's ego, the much-maligned but necessary pluck to toss off humiliation. I couldn't bear to fail—not even in a classroom exercise. My response to criticism was my response to early beatings: I shut down.

All this while, my family's tireless insistence that I marry was echoed by my psychiatrist, Dr. A, who refused to believe I had no interest in dating young men. My affairs were all with older married men. I'd come to an impasse in my therapy. Urged to work through my early traumas, I got lost in them instead. Overwhelmed, I attempted suicide.

Dr. A hospitalized me at Gracie Square. Although he had told me my diagnosis was "transference neurosis," the hospital records I later requested indicate my diagnosis as "paranoid schizophrenic, prognosis poor." Between December 9, 1959 and January 8, 1960, I received fifteen electric shock treatments (for which I was dismayed to discover my mother had given her signed consent), supplemented on alternate days by the psychotropic tranquilizer Thorazine. I was dismissed three months later.

That June I married a bass player whom I'd met the previous year. The ceremony took place in my mother's apartment. I remember dressing in her bedroom on the morning of the wedding, when she stormed in with several of her friends and, catching me in my bra, cried, "Look girls! Look what he's getting!"

Nineteen years my senior, my husband urged me to quit acting and get a regular day job. But my acting career had begun to take off. I'd been praised in the *New York Times*. My teacher, Uta Hagen, was recommending me for shows. Not long after, I became pregnant. A miscarriage in my fourth month was followed by a Mexican divorce.

Following a second suicide attempt, my career was again on hold. I was back at Gracie Square in November, 1962 awaiting an available bed at Payne Whitney for a long-term hospitalization.

Between activities at Payne Whitney I sat in my room and wrote. My pencil was confiscated: "Your writing is interfering with your therapy. You're here to relate." Admitted on April 30, 1963 as a paranoid schizophrenic, I was dismissed on April 1, 1964 as a thirty-year- old chronic undifferentiated schizophrenic with ambitions to write.

Over the next sixteen years, while on Thorazine (and other medications, including Stelazine, Haldol, Tofranil, Imipramine, and intramuscular injections of Vistaril), I remained a psychiatric patient with intervening hospitalizations. My schizophrenic diagnosis remained consistent. When my widowed mother again married and moved to Florida, I stayed in New York and, at thirty-one, with her financial help, attended college for the first time. Four years later, having earned my degree in English, I went on to Iowa City for my MFA in fiction writing. I remained in the Midwest to teach. Although gaining distance from my family helped bring them into perspective, my mother and I remained at cross purposes: I wanted to be independent; but she, in the throes of an unhappy third marriage, took refuge in overseeing my life. Her constant phone calls and unexpected visits enraged me.

In Iowa I finally found a psychologist, Melville Finkelstein, who was able to help me work through some of my difficulties. Unlike my previous therapists, he was caring, compassionate, and insightful. I eventually became a writer and full-time associate professor of English. Never again would I attempt suicide.

Into My Future

In 1977 I accepted a teaching job at the University of Kansas because of its close proximity to the Menninger Clinic (then in Topeka), where I hoped to find a lasting cure for whatever it was that ailed me. Having worked round the clock that summer on a novel that was beginning finally to take shape, I arrived exhausted in the August heat for Menninger's morning-long battery of psychological tests. As a result, the administering therapist, Dr. L, doubting I could give a coherent lecture, promptly recommended my hospitalization.

Relieved the next day to hear my new psychiatrist Dr. S soundly disagree, I went home and prepared my classes. At the end of the year my department chair informed me that my student evaluations for the fall and spring semesters had been outstanding. If I wanted to be considered for early promotion and tenure, he'd be happy to support me.

"We're doing very well," beamed Dr. S, to which I asked if he thought I'd ever be well enough to function without therapy and medication. He replied that I'd probably have to continue the therapy indefinitely; the pills would be necessary for the rest of my life.

Always I had been ready to give up, to settle. I even took a perverse pride, each time the dosage was increased, in how well I still could function. But that year things had changed: that I had done so well on heavy medication begged the question of what else was inside me: what thoughts, feelings, and possible gifts those pills were blunting. Why was I on so many? Hadn't my long-term dependence on them lowered my resistance to whatever it was that ailed me? What ailed me besides my doctor and his certainty that I was chronically ill? The realization that Dr. S had been encouraging me to remain a contented victim, that his aim, to help me thrive, was at odds with his wish to keep me in treatment, kicked in with a vengeance.

The next day I informed the Menninger Clinic that I was canceling all future appointments. That summer—in 1978, three decades ago—on a pleasure cruise with my mother and her third husband, I tossed my medications overboard. I've not seen a doctor or taken a pill since.

Let me say at great risk that nothing came into focus until I did so; at risk because it is generally believed that schizophrenia is a degenerative disease whose victims need their medication no less than diabetics their insulin. Whether I was misdiagnosed or never ill in the first place I don't know. I had to be off medications to find out, and no one would treat me without them—in or out of hospital. No one but myself.

Why did I do it? To break free from the stunning blows of the past and teach myself again to feel—love, hate, shame, even outrage from too much pain. Off medications, I remembered all I wanted to forget. Things cloudy seemed suddenly luminous and precise: I learned how and why my father's sexual abuse ruined my chances for any subsequently meaningful heterosexual relationship. I also recalled the effects of Mother and Barbara's punishments.

"Spiteful little stinker," they'd call me for doing the opposite of what I was told. The impulse to spite was still strong within me. I remembered the day I complained to my mother about my academic 'C's in high school.

"What do *you* care?" she answered. "All you want is to pass."

Is that all she thought I wanted? Or all she wanted me to want?

As soon as I knew where I stood with her, I began to do better *for spite*. Well now I'd *get* better for spite! To turn that sorry characteristic into a happy fault: to spite for a good cause became my strongest defense.

Still, my mind couldn't get at the heart of what had made my family so cruel. I wanted to make peace with them; to understand them was essential to this purpose. Was I trying too hard or in the wrong way? No sooner did I let myself rest than I stumbled onto the technique I had used as an actress to get close to characters with whom I couldn't identify: I recalled their lives and past circumstances *from their points of view*, not in order to condone but to understand why they punished me.

I saw feelingly my mother's shame over want and early poverty. An excellent student forced to drop out of school, she swept factory floors at thirteen. Someone had to put food on the table.

"I skipped grades three times," she'd cry; "I was 'A plus' in composition."

Was it any wonder she didn't encourage me to study, or attend my graduations? She'd never had one of her own.

And what of homely, pockmarked Barbara who'd locked me in closets because my needs were too sharp a reminder of hers? And, though I never doubted my sister's love, I'd delve into the roots of the conflicts that drove her to hurt as well as to help me.

Not until I saw the villains of my childhood as the misguided human beings they were did I realize the extent of their psychic pain; it was, paradoxically, the handle I needed to distance myself from my own.

The most important lesson I learned in dealing with my family during this period was to keep them out of the way *without guilt*. I regret that I didn't learn it sooner. But like everyone else, I needed family, even if it meant pretending to accede to its unfair judgments of me. If I had some of those younger years to do over, I wouldn't have visited my family quite so often. And if either my mother or sister said or did anything to hurt me, I wouldn't have hesitated to question it, or if necessary, fight back: to keep silent at my own expense only ignited the paralyzing furies within me.

If there was anything else I could have done differently, it would have been to leave home sooner. I had done so at eighteen, but when the following year my mother's second husband died, my sister said I'd have to move back. That I did so was a great mistake. It took me decades to learn that I was no slave to needs—mine *or* my family's. I had a mind as well as feelings to tend. If I'd realized that then, perhaps the healing effects of peaceful relations with my family would have come about sooner. But that it occurred at all I consider something of a miracle.

More than anything, what helped me to regain my equilibrium

after having lost it was, is, and always will be my ability to give my problems to fictional characters who define themselves by the ways in which they struggle.

Chapter 17

The Family Messiah

by Matthew Morrissey

> Editors' Introduction: *Matthew Morrissey, LMFT (co-author of this book) is a psychotherapist in private practice in San Francisco. He works with adults, teenagers, and children. He was psychiatrically hospitalized, medicated, and diagnosed with "Psychotic Disorder Not Otherwise Specified" while he was an undergraduate at Boston University in the 1990s. In his spare time he enjoys reading Plato in Ancient Greek and eating really good food. He also has a history as a sponsored amateur skateboarder.*

In 1994, late on a cold winter night just a few days after Christmas, my mother, my twelve year old sister, and I arrived at my grandmother's house in western Massachusetts. I, at twenty-one years of age, had convinced my mother and sister that it was necessary to drive there in order to save my younger brother from the evil forces that I was certain were going to kill him at any moment. In my delusional drama, my grandmother was on the good side of the cosmic forces. I felt that she possessed the "white aura" and that her house was mostly safe, except in the basement where my brother lived. I thought it was my mission to warn my brother that evil forces had crept in down there and were warping and crippling his psyche. I believed I had evolved into a higher being with psychic powers. I also sensed that the evil forces made it known that they had detected my psyche and knew that I knew they had detected it, and so were going to work all the more furiously to bring destruction down upon him. I felt like we were in a race to see who could find him first.

I spent the night trying to convince them of my beliefs, and I didn't sleep at all that night. In fact, I hadn't slept in a few days by that point. I was totally keyed up and anxious, yet at the same time dead tired. I tried to get to sleep but could not. My grandmother gave me some Benadryl for sleep but it didn't help. Every time I closed my eyes I kept coming into psychic contact with what I felt were the evil forces of the universe—and which I have since come to realize were the fantasies, wishes, and impulses in my own mind. My contact with these forces had the effect of agitating me to the point that I had to get up and move around. Sleep was impossible.

At some point my grandmother called my aunt in Boston, who was (and is) a psychiatric nurse. She tried to talk me down over the phone.

"Matthew, how are you doing right now?" she asked with concern.

"I'm fine," I answered. "I've been having the most amazing experiences over the past few days. It's like I'm finally becoming the person who I was destined to be!"

"It sounds like you're manic. Have you been sleeping?"

"Manic?" I snarled, with rising annoyance. "You don't understand. I've finally realized the truth about our family, how we treat each other, I mean. I'm going to help us all heal."

"I think you should go to the hospital, Matthew," she advised somberly.

This was too much for me to hear. "What? Go to hell!" I shouted into the phone. "You always made me feel ashamed about my mom and now you are trying to make *me* feel bad—and I don't need this in my life anymore. Goodbye!"

I hung up the phone in a rage. I remember feeling liberated by behaving in that way. Matthew, the perfect child, would no longer be so polite and accommodating. I had now recognized my true self and would brook no barriers in expression.

A little later a crisis worker called from a city organization. Apparently my aunt had contacted them about me. Things were heating up. I found myself starting to get scared, and in my sleepless state of agitation I took all this as confirmation that the evil forces had located me and were closing in. The crisis worker asked me such questions as: "Who is the president of the United States?" and "Are you thinking of hurting yourself or someone else?" I quickly recognized that I was being given an impromptu mental status exam over the phone and snapped my mind back into "mundane" reality, answering her questions calmly and accurately. Luckily I was getting my undergraduate degree in psychology at the time and so used my education as a kind of mental karate to fend her off. I put her at such ease that we made small talk and laughed together at the end of the conversation. She did, however, ask if she could call me back a little later in the day to check in on me. Realizing that if I said the wrong thing it would make me look paranoid, I told her she most certainly could.

After hanging up the phone, I got uneasy. I again considered the possibility that the crisis worker was unwittingly acting as the agent of the evil forces, who were attempting to locate my whereabouts. A disturbing scenario began to unfold in my imagination, in which it was imperative that I leave my grandmother's house for the sake of my family's safety. That way, the evil forces would follow me and leave them alone.

I thought that it was now incumbent upon me to go forth into the world and attempt to find other people who had the "white aura"— people who were psychic like me and wanted to work for good in the world by healing ourselves, our community, and the environment. In my mind I was well on my way to becoming a high priest of the white order. I felt we all had to band together to fight against the evil order—the black order—that was keeping the world under mind control and causing humans to act so irrationally and destructively. I felt that no one was strong enough to stand up against such evil on his or her own.

It was while I was considering my life as an outlaw, hunted down and persecuted by a force far more powerful than I, that I became overwhelmed with an incredible sense of loneliness and despair. I realized that I would not be able to see my family or my girlfriend again, but instead would have to sacrifice my life for the balance of the universe. I decided that I needed sleep in order to think things over.

In order to sleep, I would need something more powerful than an antihistamine like Benadryl. I decided I would have to go to the hospital where they could sedate me. I shared my decision with my mother, and she drove me straight to the emergency room. I was scared about what might happen, but kept reminding myself that I was going there only to get sleep medication. My mother encouraged this perspective, telling me that I looked exhausted and complimenting me on taking care of myself.

When we arrived at the hospital, I found that my father—who was divorced from my mother—was waiting for us outside. I remember feeling extremely awkward by him seeing me in this vulnerable state. We entered the hospital together and they stood next to me as I asked to be seen for help with my insomnia. While I was waiting to be seen, they started fighting with each other, blaming each other for what was happening to me. This was too much for my fragile nerves. I told them I wanted them to leave immediately. After making me agree that I would, in fact, wait to be seen by a doctor, they left.

When I emerged from the inpatient unit fourteen days later I was a shell of a human being. I had been put on 3mg of Risperidone soon after arrival and had mostly been ignored or talked down to by staff the whole time. I looked and felt like the living dead. My diagnosis was Psychotic Disorder Not Otherwise Specified—meaning they were sure I was psychotic but that I did not meet the criteria for a more specific psychotic disorder, like schizophrenia. However, the psychiatrists speculated that I had bipolar disorder.

I stayed at my father's apartment while I attended the intensive outpatient program at the hospital. As I was in my senior year at Boston University, and had been functioning well until my episode, the case manager in the outpatient program helped me re-enroll for my final semester. I remember my father driving me up to Boston in his truck and helping me move into my single dorm room. Before he left he looked me in the eyes and asked me if I was going to be all right. Nodding my head, I sensed his fear for the first time. I went back up into the room and collapsed onto the bare mattress, quickly drifting off into a depressive sleep.

Luckily, I ended up finding a progressive psychiatrist who helped me taper off the Risperidone. This psychiatrist referred me to a great therapist who gently helped me address the real issues in my family and my life that had brought me to such a crisis point. I addressed the role of hero and savior I was raised to play in my family, and many of the emotional conflicts that had long been brewing in my family, and that had ensnared me. I also addressed how profoundly this family tension, combined with severe lack of sleep, had unraveled my emotional balance. The whole therapy experience was so life-transforming that I decided later on to become a psychotherapist myself.

A few months after the hospitalization, I came back into conflict with my aunt, the psychiatric nurse. At this point I wanted someone in my family, anyone, to hear how hard it had been for me in the hospital, how the hospital was, in fact, more like a punishment than a place for healing. I needed someone to hear me and empathize with what I'd been through. I didn't feel safe sharing it with my parents or siblings. It was too far removed from their experience—and I didn't want to make myself so vulnerable to them about something they could not be expected to understand. I thought the person who would best understand this, of all people, was my aunt. Not only was she in the business, she also had been like a second mother to me growing up.

During one of our conversations, I told her about what I was learning in therapy: that what I had really needed at the time of my crisis was support, understanding, insight, and a good night's rest. I told her that instead of getting any of this I got hammered with antipsychotics and ignored and condescended to by the hospital staff. Upon hearing this, my aunt became incredibly irritated and defensive. She must have taken my attack on the staff's behavior as an attack on her and her profession—and the fact that she had recommended that I go to the hospital. She threw up her hands and asked me what else was she supposed to have done in that situation. I didn't have an answer for that at the time.

I felt deeply betrayed by her and a few weeks later wrote her an angry, venomous letter in retaliation. In hindsight I now realize that I took her reaction as a continuation of the hospital staff's treatment of me. Meanwhile, our relationship has never been the same, even though we have talked it over several times since then.

Looking Back With Hindsight

It is now fourteen years later. I finished school, married, and have become a private practice psychotherapist. When I look on that period of my life, with my breakdown and hospitalization, the key thing I am grateful for is that my parents supported me in taking the risk of returning to school. There is little doubt in my mind that I would have become a chronic mental patient had I not returned. It would have been so easy.

While there were many reasons for my breakdown, a clue to the most essential dynamics behind it was in the content of my delusions. If the mental health professionals in the hospital only had the training to listen in the right way, they would have been able to hear a perhaps typical yet secret story of young adulthood.

I moved away from my family to attend college in a big city. I was a pretty socially anxious young adult and I decided to major in psychology as a way to better understand myself. The problem was that my study of psychology magnified my awareness of what had gone awry in my family. When I returned home on school break, I would not only understand more and more of how I came to be so anxious as the result of my family's conflicts, but also I would see how emotionally wounded my whole family was. Truly, none of my immediate family was doing well psychologically. In moving away and beginning to grow into adulthood, I felt like I was leaving them behind—abandoning them even. The guilt was terrible and overwhelming. One summer vacation before my breakdown I had actually tried to intervene in my mother and sister's relationship by playing therapist. It was disastrous and only served to increase my anxiety. My need to save my younger brother from the "evil forces" came from a similar concern for his welfare, and a desire to help him. In reality, the forces I was trying to save him from were family dynamics.

My belief that I could help my family heal was not really new. This had been my chosen family role—possibly beginning at birth. I was to be the favored, ultra-responsible child who would keep my family in balance and redeem them through my achievements. This role certainly served me well as it provided a ready-made source of self-esteem (albeit a precarious one), and later on a nifty way of avoiding the inevitable difficulties of my own personal growth. The more I became enmeshed in their conflicts the less I could focus on myself.

It was so important for me to go back to college right after my breakdown. If I had taken a leave of absence and gone back to live with one of my parents, I would have unwittingly placed myself right at the center of the cyclone. True to my family role, I would have continued my misguided attempts to heal them at the sacrifice of my own wellbeing. The end result would not only have been massive anxiety and depression, but also a steady supply of fresh stimuli to feed my psychotic thought processes, because the only way of succeeding in such a task would have been to be a miracle worker. Getting away from my family created a spatial and temporal boundary around my experience, which helped me forget about them and focus on getting my own life together. It would be quite some time before I learned the more difficult task of maintaining psychological boundaries with others.

Looking back now, fourteen years later, I also realize that my family did come through for me in important ways even when I was in the hospital. My grandfather came to visit me every day and brought me good Italian food, while my grandmother took me out to eat when I was allowed out on day passes. My mother brought me clay and art supplies. My father visited or called me every day, simply to check up on me and listen to my concerns and worries. An aunt (not the psychiatric nurse) and step-uncle brought me a CD player with some of my favorite music. It was their simple, repeated, and thoughtful actions that made a difference. In short, they helped to restore my humanity. I shudder to think how much worse it would have been had they not come through for me. They made me feel like I had worth, at the time in my life when I thought I was worthless. I also learned in a powerful way that, dysfunctional though we might have been, my family could be counted on to show up, however imperfectly, when the going got rough.

Chapter 18

Attachments Lost And Found

by Dorothy W. Dundas

> Editors' Introduction: *Dorothy Dundas is a psychiatric survivor and longtime advocate for those in the mental health system. Diagnosed with schizophrenia in her late teens, she struggled through the mental health system, received shock therapy and antipsychotic medication, yet ultimately recovered fully. Through a number of public op-ed pieces and a poster she created from her hospital records, she has voiced her opposition to abusive psychiatric practices. Dorothy lives in the Boston area, where she raised her four children and presently runs* The Crystal Lake Express, *a local car service.*

My story of being thrust into the mental health system began on the cold, dark morning of December 4, 1960. I was nineteen years old and had left Smith College after becoming very depressed halfway through my freshman year. In my sad and confused state of mind, I overdosed on Aspirin and my parents took me to the Massachusetts General Hospital, which commenced my three-year hellish odyssey through four different mental institutions.

After a short stay at Massachusetts General Hospital I was transferred to Baldpate Hospital in Georgetown, Massachusetts, where I was diagnosed with schizophrenia. For eight weeks I was forced to undergo forty combined insulin coma/electroshock "treatments." I went through them wide awake, without any anesthesia. It was violent and it was barbaric. One terrible morning, the young girl in the bed next to me died from the shocks they had given her. She was my fragile friend and fellow traveler on this dangerous journey. On many afternoons during this vulnerable time, an attendant sexually molested me. I did not cry; I did not dare tell anyone.

We teenagers were housed in a locked cement block in the woods behind the farmhouse/"hospital" where middle-aged women who suffered from alcohol abuse were also being treated. Quite simply, I was terrified the entire time I was in that hospital. I lost my innocence, I lost my self-esteem, I was crushed as flat as a pancake, and I am lucky to be alive to tell this story today.

From Baldpate, I was transferred directly to the Menninger Clinic in Kansas where I fully expressed my outrage at being locked up against my will. That anger caused me to stop talking for weeks, to burn a hole in my arm with cigarettes, and then to be shot up with Thorazine and locked into seclusion for many days, over and over, with nothing but a mattress on the floor. There, I cried and cried and cried.

When the Menninger staff told my parents they could do nothing more for me, I was sent to the Massachusetts Mental Health Center in Boston, where I was immediately taken off the Thorazine. The side effects I was experiencing—a swollen tongue and a shuffling walk—disappeared. I remained there for another year, however, despite repeatedly trying to sign myself out every thirty days. My therapist there, a young resident doctor, sat endlessly mute, puffing on his pipe, while I sat opposite him in my own angry silence. He held all the power, and I felt withholding my voice was my only remaining option for internal survival. As his final flattening blow, he sent me to Westborough State Hospital in Massachusetts in a locked black car with two elderly custodians guarding me. I was truly on my way to a lifetime of being locked up, and I could so easily have ended up tied to my chair like the elderly women I witnessed lining the bleak hallways there. If it were not for an incredibly kind friend, Bob (a lawyer who had also been locked up at Massachusetts Mental Health Center with me), who visited me every day at Westborough and who convinced my parents to sign me out, I might still be locked up—or, more likely, dead.

My Background

In addition to being very lucky, I have always felt that the loving relationships I had within my extended family contributed to my ability to survive the atrocities of the mental health system. My wonderful grandparents and aunt lived nearby, and they showered me with adoring love and generosity from the moment I was born. The healing, long, lazy days of my summer youth were spent with them on the shores of Squam Lake in New Hampshire. Those summertimes, filled with joy and laughter and abandon, were idyllic; there, from a young age, I was given a caring and complete freedom to explore the woods and the lake with my many summer childhood friends. I believe these are the relationships and experiences which gave me internal strength and created a kernel of hope within me during the more difficult winter months and the much darker years of my hospitalizations. That hope is still within me today.

My parents were not so nurturing. I was born in 1941, during World War II, the eldest of three children. My mother cared for us at home in Cambridge, Massachusetts, while my father was away in the war. When my father returned from the war, however, there was a great deal of frightening physical and verbal conflict between him and my younger brother. This continued throughout my childhood. I remember always feeling some measure of stress and anxiety from this, and my home never felt emotionally or physically safe for me.

My parents' relationship was loving, but in their traditional marriage my mother gave over her own life and whatever needs or aspirations she might have had to supporting my father, both at home and in his work. They led busy lives and were often out of town, once leaving me for three months when I was three months old and again leaving all three of us in the care of a nanny for three months when I was six. I missed my mother and wished she had been home to protect us from the nanny's harsh, even cruel, punishments. From this point on, I slipped into a cautious relationship with my parents. My refuge was with my grandparents and aunt and at school, where I had many good friends and always received positive attention for my natural athletic abilities.

Despite what might appear to have been a certain degree of resilience gifted to me from those nurturing summers, my relationship with my immediate family was severely tested during and after my hospitalizations. Wearing my favorite red dress, I rode out in silence to Baldpate Hospital in the front seat between my parents. I had been told I was going to a sanitarium. I thought that I must be suffering from tuberculosis, and from the moment of realizing where I was, when they took away my belt, I felt abandoned and completely frightened. After the electroshocks began, I could not imagine how my parents would allow me to be so brutalized, and why they were not coming to rescue me. While at the Menninger

Clinic, I remember lying in seclusion for days and days and days and crying endlessly for my mother, in desperation for having been abandoned into these supposed "healing" prisons of violence. I suspect that some of my sorrow and desperation was the reliving of her absences during my early childhood. And, although my mother did visit me occasionally over the course of the three years, all of my energy went into struggling to survive within that violent medical war zone, and I became further and further isolated from thoughts of my family and whatever small intimacies we might previously have shared.

Nothing in my life had prepared me for where I found myself. And, as I learned, my world centered entirely around the hospital ward, my fellow patients, and the doctors and nurses who may have thought they were helping, but who were, in fact, hurting us all. They were crushing us both emotionally and physically. In this process, I ended up learning a complex set of behaviors which called upon my use of silence, anger, and self-abuse to maintain that small kernel of hope within my soul. These sometimes unconscious and out-of-my-control choices did not always serve me well, and when all else failed, and when I became too exhausted, I would slip into the deepest of sorrows (in seclusion and restraints and heavily medicated). But I was alive, and survival was almost always my primary goal from the minute my roommate was killed by the shocks. There was simply no room for my family on this dangerous and lonely journey.

After finally landing in Westborough State Hospital, I spent my days making and remaking my bed in the darkness at 6:00 a.m. so the nurses could bounce a quarter on it, scraping garbage along with other patients in the kitchen, trying to console the elderly women tied to their chairs, and nervously sitting in the dayroom waiting for my heroic and dear friend, Bob, to arrive in the early evenings. Then, one cold morning, while I was scraping, a nurse told me she was taking me to Dr. Sharp. I had no idea who he was or what was about to happen. She led me through corridors to a huge office where I was presented to Dr. Morris L. Sharp, superintendent, *and* to my parents. I was completely dumbfounded and very nervous about where they might be planning to send me next—perhaps for brain surgery, a lobotomy? I trusted no one. Dr. Sharp explained that he would give me permission to go home if I met two of his conditions. First, I had to promise to go to secretarial school, starting on Monday, two days later, and second, I had to return to see him every Saturday morning. Although I felt simultaneously trapped and relieved and betrayed, I would have agreed to almost anything to regain my freedom. At last my parents had finally rescued me—and again, sitting silently between them, I rode home to begin the rest of my life.

Although my transition from hospital to home was incredibly liberating (I was out and free to breathe or eat or sleep or walk whenever I wished), it was also very difficult. Everything looked too bright and the everyday sounds were too loud. It seemed as if I were living in a parallel universe to that of everyone around me. I went through all of the motions of daily life. I ate, I slept, and I went to secretarial school and learned to type 120 words per minute (this was my mother's dream for me as she had been my father's secretary before they were married).

On Saturdays my parents drove me back out to Westborough to see the frightening Dr. Sharp. I told him only what I thought would keep me free: facts of going to school, nothing at all personal. I walked through my fragile little life on tiptoe feeling as though a scarlet letter were stitched upon my breast for all to see: "S" for schizophrenic. The fear that I might make one misstep and end up in the hospital again controlled all of my behavior. I was shattered, but I was a model of good behavior. To their credit, my parents were kind. My father drove me to school, my mother cooked dinner. But at home we were all walking on eggshells; no one ever mentioned a word about where I had been or what it had been like for me or for them. No one. Myself included. This is true to this very day, forty-six years later. I have simply never been willing to go into that black hole which is full of so much deep hurt and anger. Sometimes, it really is better to leave dark nightmares in the provinces of dreamy sleep.

After several months of living at home and going to secretarial school, I was able to find an apartment with roommates and a job. Although I was still angry at my parents for having locked me up, I was not able to express my feelings openly and needed to be away from them. I have heard it said that my family's decision to lock me up is what families did back in the 1960s and earlier. The fact is, this is not what all families did with their depressed or rebellious children. Some, like David Oaks, were rescued. His mother traveled far to demand his freedom from a psychiatric hospital. And I have heard other stories like his. Probably in part because my family did not fight to rescue me and find a more compassionate form of help, my relationships within my family became more and more distant. I needed that distance.

Looking back, I cannot imagine how I lived through that time. I remember simply putting one foot in front of the other, taking tiny baby steps towards being more fully in a life of my own. I became even more self-conscious when, because of the electroshocks, my front teeth started to turn brown and finally fell out while I was eating a sandwich. It was embarrassing; I felt no one would love me. Getting my front teeth replaced helped significantly. I told very few people about where I had spent the last few years; even so, I was to learn a lot more about the pain of discrimination. One of my roommates heard that I had been in a mental hospital, and she was so frightened that she moved out the very next day. That hurt. At the same time, I was also becoming close to a seemingly nice boyfriend who was a medical student. He also became aware through friends that I had been locked up. He asked me directly if this were true; I told him it was. He left that evening and never called again. Those experiences caused me to be much more cautious about sharing myself with others.

Fortunately, at about this time I was referred to a wonderful new therapist, Dr. Lee Macht. He was completely different from any of the doctors who had previously sat mute with me. He smiled, he had a sparkle in his eye, and he saved my life in all possible ways. He told me that he did not think I had ever been "crazy." He told me that he thought I had been behaving understandably in self-defensive ways to protect myself in what he described as my own "private holocaust." He encouraged me to go back to college, helped me write my college essay, and wrote a recommendation for me. He was the first person truly to listen to me. He believed in me; he gave me back that kernel of hope which had been almost totally crushed. Later, he also encouraged me to write about my experiences for the newspaper. Quite simply, he was a warm, gentle and encouraging mother to me.

With his support, I blossomed. I made friends and I graduated from college. During this time, I also married, and my husband and I shared in the raising of our four wonderful children. After twelve years, however, our marriage ended, and I became a full-time single parent. Also, with joy and disbelief, at this time I also met my true fellow travelers—courageous members of the Mental Patients Liberation Front in Boston. In addition to Dr. Lee Macht and my children, the members of this organization turned out to be the people who further positively changed my life. We shared a language and a set of feelings similar to those described by Holocaust survivors and veterans of combat battle units. This connection to people who had traveled my same path through violent hospitalizations gave me confidence, encouraged me again to tell my story to educate and try to prevent others from going through similar experiences. It is important for families to recognize that once their family member has been so violated, and he or she has not been protected or rescued from those inhumanities, it is very difficult ever to regain any real sense of trust. Perhaps if my parents had been more genuinely nurturing, if all of our family had received caring support during my youth, we might have had a chance to become closer. I suspect that my hospitalization was simply the last straw in a series of smaller childhood leavings, insensitivities, and lapses in parental judgment to which I responded by turning elsewhere for love and care. For me, this turned out to be a necessary and healing choice. I have been strong, happy, and healthy for a long, long time—forty-six years.

Today, as I write this, my father is no longer living; towards the end of his life we made a gentle and silent peace. My sister and I visit with my mother and show her the kindnesses which very elderly mothers deserve in spite of her earlier choices in regard to my care. Now, along with my dear children, grandchildren, sister, and many long-devoted friends in my home community, my family includes hundreds encircling one another in trust and support.

Chapter 19

Life After Family

by Will Hall

> Editors' Introduction: *Will Hall is the co-founder of* Freedom Center, *a free, volunteer, peer-run community for psychiatric survivors in Northampton, Massachusetts.* Freedom Center *supports informed choice and self-determination regarding medication and other treatments, and offers holistic alternatives including support groups, acupuncture, writing workshops, yoga classes, and public education. Will is also a co-coordinator of* The Icarus Project *and host of* Madness Radio *(www.madnessradio.net), syndicated on the Pacifica FM network. Will was hospitalized and diagnosed with schizophrenia in his twenties, and has been medication free since then. He is presently a counselor in Portland, Oregon and is working toward his Master's degree in psychology at the Process Work Institute.*

"...what is usually called hypnosis is an experimental model of a naturally occuring phenomenon in many families. In the family situation, however, the hypnotists (the parents) are already hypnotised (by their parents) and are carrying out their instructions, by bringing their children up to bring their children up..."

"I consider that the majority of adults (including myself) are or have been, more or less, in a post-hypnotic trance, induced in early infancy: we remain in this state until—when we dead awaken, as Ibsen makes one of his characters say, we shall find that we have never lived."

-R.D. Laing, *The Politics of the Family*

In 1979, when I was thirteen years old, my mother volunteered at one of the first rape crisis centers in Florida. She was on-call and they gave her a pager, one of the early kinds, so they could contact her whenever a woman came to the center needing help. I had never seen a pager before. It was about seven inches tall and didn't do anything except glow with a steady red light until it was activated. Then it went off with a loud electronic whoop. When Mom went to bed she put the pager on the center of the kitchen counter, and it sat there all night, like a small ticking bomb.

It wasn't until years later that my mother's pager took on a special significance for me. I always loved science fiction and secret agents, and here was an advanced technology hinted at in movies that had taken up residence in our family. It waited until some unknown moment came, listening electronically for a distant invisible signal. And then suddenly it exploded our entire house into a panic—one moment quiet and still and the next screeching like a siren with its message that we were in the midst of an emergency.

When I was finally hospitalized in my mid-twenties and given a diagnosis of schizophrenia, the alarm was sounding for me.

Growing up was a slow motion, silent crisis. Both my parents are trauma survivors, and by that I don't mean they lived through one incident of violence, I mean they endured lives of repeated brutality. Dad is a veteran of the Korean War, and he was shot and beaten, killed strangers and watched friends die, spent time in prison, and underwent torture. He is such a complicated man that no sketch could outline his personality. Without warning he became friendly and kind, then brooding or enraged. He berated my mother, brother, and me cruelly, then praised us for our accomplishments. He allowed us great freedom in one moment, and demanded complete control the next. He taught independence and resilience, but wasn't there when we needed him. He lashed out, then gave us gifts, talked about books and movies, then put us down for having opinions of our own. He kept his psychiatric history and electroshock treatments hidden, then told me one day, "I was in mental hospitals. You knew that." We were never sure if he was at war or peace.

My mother had her own, more hidden weapons. She cut with a look in her eyes, silenced us with a tone in her voice, turned cold when we sought warmth. She was orphaned as a little girl, then survived sexual mistreatment that also included torture. She didn't know how to give me, her first son, privacy and independence, and turned to me for the intimacy she didn't find in her husband. Mom's inner strength at being mixed Choctaw Indian earned some respect from my dad, and my brother and I were taught to be proud of our indigenous ancestry, but she was also ridiculed for expressing her own intellect and feelings. Dad would sometimes say, "Your mother is very special," and I could hear, faintly, an echo of the time he was in love with her.

I wouldn't call what my parents did fighting, because he crushed her so utterly. But I also saw her venom scar and burn him. They circled each other, scraped and clawed, shouted, and then fell silent for days. When my dad and mom met and started a family, they found in each other a shelter from their violent pasts. Then the shelter collapsed around them.

In these ruins my brother and I kept our heads down. We weren't very friendly, and spent most of our time together mistrustful and competitive. When we did challenge our parents it just erupted into vicious and overwhelming scenes. My brother was able to stand up and yell back; I just collapsed and froze. I don't know which was better. There were no other witnesses to what was going on, and it was only years later as adults that we could reassure each other that, no, we didn't imagine it, and yes, it was that bad.

The pager knew something about our family. It watched and listened, and when it sounded its alarm the crisis wasn't just out there in someone else's life; the crisis was here at home. We lived our lives in a trance, showing up for school and sitting in front of television and going to the mall, all while hypnotically induced to believe that the tremors and smoke of conflict surrounding us were normal. When in the middle of the night we heard the shrieking pager, it was us it was trying to wake up.

Even fleeing to the West Coast for school I couldn't escape. I struggled with what I called my depression, but it was much more than that. I would fall silent for days, hide from others, hear voices in my head attacking me, feel malevolent entities tracking me down. My mind became so unmoored that I climbed in and out of the window to leave my apartment, afraid my roommates were trying to hurt me. I saw crowds watching from the rooftops, heard whispered conspiracies on the other side of the wall, froze in terror when the devil called my name. I walked again and again to the Golden Gate Bridge and stared at the water below, and I stood in traffic holding a torn sign inscribed with coded messages. I spiraled deeper into my own madness.

In the locked ward of Langley Porter Psychiatric Institute I underwent tests and interviews, observations and questionnaires. At a solemn meeting with the psychiatrist it was finally announced that I had a severe psychiatric illness. It was another spell, another trance, this time cast by doctors. Your genes are faulty; your brain chemistry, your biology. You will never recover. You will always need medication. You cannot regain control of your life: give up your dreams, give up your ambitions. I felt perversely relieved, as if by becoming a patient and being diagnosed as mentally ill I was fulfilling an elaborate suicidal wish.

At the news that I was in a mental hospital, my father blamed recreational drugs while my mother blamed my father. A psychiatric diagnosis is a blame sponge: guilt is gathered up and put on a disordered brain or predisposed genes, guilt no one wants spilled on themselves. I don't blame my family. I don't blame any family. Trauma and violence sprawl across generations and extend out into the world. I don't know if blame would really help anyone at this point.

My mother was in therapy and she realized my father's violent past was taking a terrible toll on our lives together. But she couldn't see her own role and was helpless to change it, to talk, to break the spell we were all under. To this day I have never had a conversation with my father, mother, or brother about being diagnosed with schizophrenia. Years of trying to speak only led back into my worst mental states. And so at different times in my life I've broken contact from them entirely. When I do make plans to visit I hope for a snowstorm to cancel the flight, or some other reason not to go. I live in a kind of exile from my family, and a silent and unbreakable taboo is still in place against who I am. We continue trapped in the codes and dramas of our past. The alarm keeps going off.

I spent a year looking for help in the public mental health system before I began, slowly, to look within myself. My freedom and recovery eventually came through trusted friends and support groups, holistic health and acupuncture and nutrition, meditation and spiritual discipline. I stopped taking psychiatric drugs, and I stopped believing in the diagnosis I was given. I've gained enough clarity to make a fragile but lasting peace with madness, and live with my wild mind, voices, and altered states of consciousness. I now trust that when the demons come, the angels will soon also have their turn.

Recovery for me has also meant leaving my father, mother, and brother behind. I do know many people who have confronted their family, heard the alarm and shaken themselves awake from the trance, and finally found in their parents the warmth and strength they needed to come back to life. My family still exerts a diabolical hold over me. When I am in contact with them it's as if I leave my present self and return to the past. The power of that generations-old trance remains. My family has never woken up, and might not ever wake up.

Today I work as a mental health advocate and counselor, and I get calls and emails from people searching for an answer different from what they've been told by doctors and TV ads. When parents contact me, desperate to help their sons and daughters, I do hold out the possibility of change. I believe these frightened and traumatized fathers and mothers can grow and become a source of freedom for their children. I tell them that families can heal and that people can recover.

For me, my family is still something I protect myself from. The pager sits there in the middle of the kitchen counter, waiting to sound its alarm.

Chapter 20

My Family and I

by Joanne Greenberg

> Editors' Introduction: *Joanne Greenberg, DHL is the world-renowned author of the bestselling novel* I Never Promised You A Rose Garden, *a slightly fictionalized account of her recovery from schizophrenia. From 1948 to 1952 Joanne was a patient of Dr. Frieda Fromm-Reichmann at the psychiatric hospital Chestnut Lodge. Born in 1932, Joanne began hearing auditory hallucinations well before her teen years, and also experienced visual hallucinations and significant disorganized thinking. She created her own language, Irian, immortalized in Rose Garden as the language of Yr. Joanne is also the author of sixteen other books of fiction (including* In This Sign *and* Of Such Small Differences), *and has worked for nearly twenty years as a professor of anthropology at the Colorado School of Mines. Prior to that she worked as a sixth grade teacher and an emergency medical technician. She has been married for over fifty years, and is the mother of two adult sons.*

I had been mentally ill since the age of five, seriously since I was ten, which would have been 1942. I saw a child psychiatrist then. He was not a good person and I was able to stop seeing him. My symptoms led to another try when I was thirteen and the doctor, a good man, told me that I was very ill and should be in a hospital, but that the one he wanted for me wouldn't take anyone my age. He asked me if I could hang with him until I was sixteen. I said I thought I could. I saw that doctor once a week until my sixteenth birthday, but I don't think I could have hung on much longer. His validation of my deep knowledge that there was something very wrong in my life was very helpful. My family imputed my withdrawal and general lifelessness to the sensitivity of the creative spirit. They had no expectations for me because I think they had few for themselves. In some ways that was good or would be later, when I was in the hospital.

My parents took me to Chestnut Lodge in Maryland, where I could receive psychotherapy. There were no psychotropic medications in those days. I was in the hospital from September 25, 1948, until February, 1951, with two trips back to New York, and was an outpatient until 1953.

Prior to going to the hospital, I had the usual dysfunctional childhood. In those days, people of our class had caretakers, nurses, governesses, etc. My governess was an unstable woman, which added to my burdens. I had been born with a physical anomaly that made me unable to control my bladder, so I was always wet and smelly and people laughed at me, and my father called me down about it. When I was five I had a series of very painful procedures that corrected this anomaly. The hospital people denied that I was feeling pain and promised me, between one procedure and another, that the next one would be painless and would be done on my doll. The stretching of my sphincter, which has given me trouble all my life, contributed to my mental disorder, and it was around this time that I began hearing voices. No one in my family ever spoke of what had happened to me.

As for my relationship with my parents, I have good memories of my father, but they are very old. When I was six or seven he developed a crippling ulcer. At that time, there was no treatment for stomach ulcers. He drew away from us into his pain. My mother was psychologically burdened by living in a house she hated, in Brooklyn, which she hated, and in a life, with the exception of her relationship with my father, that she hated. I don't remember seeing much of her, although she was sometimes full of fun, but she was blighted in some way. This caused her to be depressed or absent. She had no friends until we moved to New York and then her friendships were intense but sporadic, one person at a time, until some word or slight made her drop the person.

I have a sister who is five years younger than I and was cute and pretty and everything I wasn't. I was supposed to be the brilliant one—special. The kids in school knew that I was mentally ill and left me alone, keeping their distance. I was sent to an anti-Semitic camp each summer after I was six and was left unprotected. Everyone knew what I was. Camp was two months long, and was 24/7. What everyone thought was wonderful and liberating was for me frightening and isolating. I never talked with my parents about what I went through at camp. All the while, I was said to be brilliant. My family felt good about my writing and it was all I could do not to confuse it with my self, which is the bane of many, if not most, writers.

Most of my extended family didn't know about my illness or hospitalization. They had been told I was in a private school. My cousin spent some time in NPI (the New York Psychiatric Institute), but I don't know about his treatment. The five-year difference between my sister and me meant that she wasn't much help to me, and from my side I was afraid of damaging her. Because of my illness, my parents slept with their door open and my mother gave up her singing lessons and concertizing. They wanted me well, but these adjustments didn't help. However, they stood by the two-plus years that I was going to my doctor in New York and the three years plus outpatient treatment that I was at Chestnut Lodge, a significant financial commitment. On my two visits home everyone was very careful, but I had to keep visiting my family because that was what was expected. My mother always called her sister and her mother every day and I was expected to call or visit every day.

How I Dealt with My Family

I never developed any skills at dealing with my family—we just muddled through. I knew in some way that I had to separate from them because they were unable to help me, and after an initial shock—that I would never be the person they wanted me to be—they seemed to realize this also. My therapist helped me in my realization and since I had a year as a five-times-a-week outpatient, I stayed in Maryland and then in Washington, D.C., far from New York where the family lived. I went to remedial school for my G.E.D., and then to secretarial school, and finally to American University. Summers I worked at various jobs, which gave me some of the social experience I so desperately needed. Having been sick for so long, I had to start from ground zero to learn the necessary social skills. I spent only one summer in New York.

Maybe the most successful thing I did during that period was done without conscious planning, but by demonstration. I slowly proved to myself that I could live like other people. I sang in a church choir as I was recovering in the hospital, and later at Tanglewood. I worked at the Washington, D.C. airport and as a waitress and then worked on the Navajo Reservation in Arizona. I went to the University of Colorado one summer and shocked my therapist, who was in Santa Fe, where she owned a house, by showing up as a horse herder in the Santa Fe Fiesta. I went to London University, got engaged, got jilted, cried, and in general had a wonderful time.

I think the best thing that helped my relationship with my parents happened when they saw me succeeding, even though it wasn't the way they had planned for me or the way most girls did it at the time. My father was worried about my ability to live a normal life. I knew I could never do that in New York, which I hated, not only as the place where I had been at my sickest, but also as a city, itself. There is something about cities that makes me feel clumsy, graceless, and diminished. Where one lives isn't usually thought of as a factor in becoming or staying healthy, but for me, it certainly was. I've known people here in Colorado, where I have lived for the past fifty-three years, who hate it and get sick physically, and psychologically, because of their unhappiness. When I came out of New York I felt full-grown for the first time.

The way that I learned the skills of relating better with my family mostly involved trial and error, blundering, and a couple of returns to the hospital when I: a) confused problems with symptoms; and b) couldn't believe I was who I was turning into. In the hospital I had the chance to reevaluate my life and my relationships with my parents.

In terms of advice to others, I will speak about what I might have done differently. I would reassure my family constantly that they need not be afraid of my illness or my therapy, that the exploration of family secrets in therapy would never shame them, that their errors were errors of love, most often, and that they had done the best they could under the circumstances. I would tell them not to be afraid of me and my differences, that my differences wouldn't humiliate them, but might instead bring them rewards, as mine, indeed, did. My having had appropriate therapy made them much more open in their own lives and more open to seeing it as an option for other members of the family.

To be fair, I made my share of errors in dealing with my family. I didn't share much of my inner life with them, fearing that my social struggle, my loneliness in the learning I had to do, would make them too nervous. I didn't let them know how tough I was, and when I did, I didn't get much credit for it. The plaudits came from friends, or, later, my husband. I did tell my mother that being better didn't mean that I would not have weaknesses and faults. I often had to check out my reality with people I trusted, whether what I was thinking and feeling was appropriate for the situation. Confidence has to be built over the years, especially when one's reality has been so often challenged.

When I look back on those early years of my recovery, in my early twenties, I think of other things I would do differently. I think I would try to treat my family a little bit as patients—encouraging them to go out to places in the city. I would also wish to open up to my father a little more than I did, and to talk with my sister more. In many ways I kept myself closed off from them, perhaps in self-protection.

In some ways it wasn't easy being a member of my family, and this made my recovery more difficult. I could never be the person my parents wanted me to be and I felt that both of them loved me but wanted me to be different. My father needed support he wouldn't let me give him. He was lost in my mother's very judgmental family. I was supposed to be a genius, but genius is a separating idea and concentrates on many negative images—egotism, dramatics, and hypersensitivity. The designation makes one sicker—and did for me. My parents never knew anyone like me. That's why the designation of schizophrenia was so liberating for me—it isn't for most people. The diagnosis meant that I had been right all along—there was something terribly amiss in me, something that had to be faced and dealt with. The patchings and the excuses and the faking could fall away and what was real could come forward. I'm glad my sister was around to be the "normal" one; it helped take the pressure off me—and later, she was someone I could test my reality with.

My parents, however, did some things that were very helpful to me in my recovery. They endured and they let go. They tried to understand when I told them that healthy and normal were two different things. They also trusted me enough to let me stay in a small rural hotel for a month during part of the last six months of my hospitalization, and they supported my hospitalization and the therapy all the long years of it. Also, they let me go to college and spend summers away from what was a pretty airless environment of family responsibility.

In terms of what I personally did to retain or regain my family equilibrium, I never had an equilibrium to begin with. I was never socially viable or had any healthy past I could relate to. I stopped growing inside after the age of ten, so I had to learn it all from scratch—and from my last six months of hospitalization where I was passionate to learn all I could from the nurses, students, aides, and other patients. I was lucky in that I was not in an adolescent unit, such as they have now. I saw the full panoply of human beings and was able to get advice and support from many of the other patients, where I don't think adolescents would have been able to help.

But what most gave me strength in dealing with my family was Albert, my husband, whom I married when I was twenty-three. My family's strength was defensive, using wit rather than humor. In our own ways, we loved each other. This was what made breaking away so difficult. We knew that we couldn't live close, my husband and I, so we moved to Colorado. My family would have ripped my husband to shreds.

Chapter 21

Patch's Story

by Patch Adams

> Editors' Introduction: *Hunter "Patch" Adams, M.D. is a physician, social activist, citizen diplomat, professional clown, and international leader in the field of alternative models of health care. In 1972 he founded the* Gesundheit! Institute, *based in Arlington, Virginia, where he promotes a medical model not funded by insurance policies. Patch was hospitalized three times for psychiatric problems in the 1960s, but found his way out—with his family's help—and has since recovered fully. Patch's life was the template for the 1998 film* Patch Adams, *starring Robin Williams.*

I am sixty-three years old. I grew up on Army bases—mostly outside of the United States. I was most fortunate to have a fabulous mother who showered me with love and gave me self-esteem. She filled me with a lifelong interest in everything by developing my senses of wonder and curiosity.

I am a nerd and school was easy. At the age of sixteen, my father died from war and we moved back to the United States to Virginia to an all-white public school. I immediately got involved in the Civil Rights Movement and was ostracized and beaten up often. I felt isolated and wept for the realization that our country was fake, religion was fake, and that the adult world was not about compassion and generosity. I wanted to die. I didn't want to live in a world of violence and injustice.

I was psychiatrically hospitalized three times from 1962-63. The last was on a locked ward. In retrospect it was the best people-watching ever. I noticed that the staff didn't seem any happier than the patients. I was placed on Librium and hated it. The psychiatrist had no idea how to be with a teenager. Each hospitalization was ten to fourteen days. On the third hospitalization it hit me: you don't kill yourself, you make revolution. So I've been devotedly working for peace and justice since. I also began to realize that the patients were mostly different than I. Every day my mom came and said, "You're not crazy." Friends came and we enjoyed checking the hospital out. I realized that I had love and friends and that if I held them in my consciousness I could not suffer. I found overwhelming loneliness in the patients I spoke with. I claim that at that time I dove into the ocean of gratitude and never found the shore. I decided to serve humanity in medicine (I've been a free doctor for thirty-eight years) and to make myself into an instrument for peace and justice by deciding to be happy every day for the rest of my life. By living intentionally, I've been disgustingly happy for forty-five years. I've had no personal suffering these forty-five years.

My mental hospitalization had very little effect on my relationships with my friends or family. We jokingly called me "Psycho Patch." I was instantly full of life—to explore everything. I began a habit of reading one to two hundred books a year, which I have continued to the present. Maybe I stayed crazy, but it's a kind of crazy I celebrate. For me, the hospitalization is mostly a memory of what not to do for the mentally ill—and has made me a family doctor unwilling to prescribe psycho-pharmaceuticals. The hospitalizations have also helped me relate much better to troubled folk—to give them hope for change. I now teach living from intention—choosing your life's course and going with it.

I never had to really learn to "deal" with my family. My dad was dead, my mother loved me unconditionally, and my brother was a deep playmate. My brother works with me now and has most of his life. By being happy, engaged, and consistently friendly, I have found it easy to have great relationships with family. My mom lived in our commune the last year of her life. I'm sure I've stayed crazy—and I'm most comfortable crazy.

> "A man needs a little madness, or else he never dares cut the rope and be free."
>
> —Nikos Kazantzakis, *Zorba the Greek*

I found out that if you find friends and collect them together that this too is family. And among this family you have a freedom to be as crazy as you dare. So family is a nest. For this reason, I found that it felt right to live communally. This was the most important decision of my life. This family is like an in-house study, a work-in-progress. And as you feel this collective love of friends—and self-love and freedom—it is not possible to be mentally troubled. The engaged connection that family can be *is* mental health. It can come from friends, nature, arts, and gods. As I found I could "make me"—intentionally be the *me* I wanted to be—every moment, I could actually feel and act as if all people are my family. I fell in love with humanity.

My advice to people? Turn off the TV. Think about and explore things you are drawn to. Anything. There are many wise books. Have all friends agree that the goal is yummy love to and for everyone. Relax. Decide exactly who you will be and be it. Most important, realize that the global community is hurting, crumbling, and needs your help now. Become an activist.

Maybe mental illness is a healthy response to our fucked up system, hell-bent on extinction. (That is a paraphrase of Freud from *Civilization and Its Discontents*.) Stop whining and be grateful—and work until everyone and nature are cared for and women are safe. And no one is hungry.

Are there errors I have made? None. I think when you decide to be loving, friendly, and goofy—and never to harm—that errors are just other explorations. I learned to get closer and closer to people and found that errors helped that process greatly. Silence is much more dangerous. Same with hurt. What one calls hurt I see as opportunity, the potential for deeper understanding. This opportunity is hard to grasp for people who lack self-esteem. In my four-hour initial interview with new patients, I find less than three percent have self-esteem (that basic "I love me"—that I clearly learned from my mother). My advice: fall in love with you.

What did my family (my direct family, then extended family, then friends, community, and the world of people) do best for me? They, then to present, lavish me with friendship. Encouragement, foundation, and a launching pad. My fantasies can be so much bigger with family than by myself. They let me be a GREAT APE. Everything I've done has been with family. *Total* freedom from suffering comes simply by thinking of friends. My first costume (that I made) was a gorilla. The second was an asshole costume. Since 1972 I have used both countless times in public with friends. Yum!

The best thing that helped (and helps) me recover, as I've hinted at, is to "make me." I disciplined my thinking to be focused on making the exact *me* I wanted—and decided—to be. It could be called acting intentionally. It was equally important that I first chose to be a funny, loving, caring person, 24/7. Being that has made and sustained everything else. When I wanted to kill myself, I still loved myself and life. I didn't know that I was to spend that funny, loving, and caring person's life working for peace and justice. As soon as I chose to live a revolution of loving, I didn't have to find something lost: I had to discover revolution. Working for peace and justice *is* mental health. I didn't need any strength in dealing with my family: they were my strength. One way I could tell (when I was an active family doc) whether a patient really felt like the member of a family was to see if he or she lost or gained strength from their family. Our home hospital was family to many—the main draw for coming here.

Yea life.

Chapter 22

Coming Off Psychiatric Drugs, Coming Into Myself

By Gianna Kali

> *Editors' Introduction: Gianna Kali is a psychiatric survivor, mental health advocate, ex-social worker, and internet blogger who writes on psychiatric advocacy and safe and healthy withdrawal from psychiatric medication. Her blog,* Beyond Meds: Alternatives to Psychiatry *(www.bipolarblast.wordpress.org), is read by thousands of people each month. In the course of her journey through the mental health system, where she was diagnosed with bipolar disorder, she was on a total of thirty-nine different psychiatric medications.*

My Journey Through the Psychiatric System

In 1985, when I was a nineteen year old sophomore at UC Berkeley, I began experimenting with illicit drugs—most notably hallucinogens, and specifically LSD, mushrooms, and MDMA (Ecstasy). After one of my acid trips I didn't "come down." I simply stayed in a state that was similar to being high on a hallucinogen and I started having what I now view as a spiritual emergency. This chaotic but exciting state of self-discovery landed me in a psychiatric ward against my will. My "psychosis" consisted of religious delusions along with other ideas that didn't quite fit consensual reality. I feel that had I had someone to listen to me and work through my delusions in a safe place I would have simply had a washout period and I then would have been fine. I had never lost touch with consensual reality prior to hallucinogen use.

Instead I was arrested for trespassing when I refused to leave a psychic institute where I had gone hoping for spiritual assistance. I knew very well I needed help, but I did not imagine myself psychiatrically diseased. The people at the psychic institute asked me to leave and I did not. At this point I was merely trespassing. I did not threaten anyone. All I did was plant myself on their floor against their wall. I was picked up by policemen and thrown down the stairs when I refused to move. When I picked myself off the ground I tried to get away from the violent police officers but was instead cattle-tied, ankles to wrists in the back of their car. They took me to the first of three hospitals I would stay in over the next three months, for about a week each time. I was strapped down, put in isolation and injected with neuroleptics multiple times.

The reason I was never in the hospital for long was that I always requested a hearing and once I was in front of a judge I could convince them I was okay. I was basically pretty lucid and could figure out what the judge wanted to hear.

Nonetheless, I had not figured out that hallucinogens were not a good idea for me and I repeated the trip to the hospital three times after ingesting hallucinogens. I dearly wanted to communicate with god and it seemed the illicit drugs were allowing me to do this.

After the final hospitalization I figured out that I should stop doing the hallucinogens and stopped the revolving-door practice and remained free of the hospital. I continued to go to school after a semester's break and for the most part I stopped taking the medications the psychiatrists prescribed. I took low doses of a medication to help me sleep but did not take the lithium the psychiatrists wanted me to take for what they had labeled manic-depression. This was before the "bipolar disorder revolution."

While in the hospital I was very much abused and humiliated and told I was sick with a disease that I would have for life. A psychiatrist who is now very prominent in the California government making mental health policy yelled at me once, truly screamed, that if I did not take meds for the rest of my life I would die. Even though I did not follow his orders at that point, that moment remains in my mind the moment of trauma that undermined my belief in myself and ultimately led me to my decision to succumb to treatment later on. This same doctor who yelled at me also broke my confidentiality and told his brother, whom I happened to live with in student housing, details about my diagnosis and hospitalization. Because of this, news got around to everyone I knew.

A few years later I felt depressed and visited a holistic doctor. She gave me excitatory amino acids which are often used as a natural remedy for depression. They made me "hypomanic." They did not make me psychotic, nor did I lose touch with consensual reality, but the feeling was reminiscent of when I had lost control on psychedelic drugs. At that point I did not know that amino acids could trigger this and so I imagined that the doctors must be right. I was sick. I was diseased. As long as illicit drugs had induced my manias I felt that the doctors couldn't call me crazy, but now that as far as I knew nothing at all had triggered my "crazy" energy, I believed I was defective and would need drugs for the rest of my life. I was running scared and in my quest to avoid hospitalization at all costs I ran straight to a psychiatrist and asked that I be put on psychiatric drugs. In my mind staying out of the hospital was akin to staying alive. I did not understand at that point that medications also take your life away.

What follows is not pretty. I was on drugs for the next fifteen years and now in the last five I have been withdrawing from them. I was put on six different drugs at very high doses—double and triple the usual doses. I ended up on so many drugs not because I had a mental illness that needed treating but because I was put on additional drugs to treat side effects of the other drugs I was taking. I am now off all but one of these drugs. Withdrawal is a slow and agonizing process after all these years. All my emotions and psychic dysfunction that I could have been working out all these years had been numbed in place.

I am working towards withdrawing from the final psychotropic. I have no doubt I will make it at this point. I've also learned that there is nothing wrong with my mind. I am off all neuroleptics and mood stabilizers and my mind is fine though I have a lot of emotional work still to do. The drugs, unfortunately, have wreaked havoc on my body and I am very physically ill. They have poisoned my body.

My Family's Role During My Hospitalization

Where was my family in all this? While I was in the hospital my mother was constantly worried and ever-present in a smothering way that was most unhelpful—though she meant well and I understand that now. My mother by her nature and to this day worries incessantly. While I was growing up, this habit of hers translated in my mind into a total lack of trust in my ability to make choices for myself and infused me with a sense of insecurity. My mother was also completely controlled by my father, which further created a negative relationship between us. For that reason, in my vulnerable state while hospitalized I felt that she was toxic to me. Indeed, I had to get away from her for a good long time as well, though her love for me was great and real.

Besides my mom who was at the hospital quite often I remember only one of my brothers visiting once, but he came all the way from Italy so that was significant. My father visited only once. I don't remember my sister or other brother visiting at all—and they lived in the very near vicinity. I don't remember anyone being helpful throughout the hospitalization process, and though my brother's brief visit from Italy was touching it was not extended enough to help.

My aunt, however, was very nice and supportive and let me live with her for four months while I recovered from the insult of hospitalization. Living with my mom's overbearing worry was not an option for me and I'm sure living with my aunt was key to my getting back on my feet. After living with her I went back to school and, with some disruptions, completed my degree. I will always be grateful for the great kindness my aunt showed me during that very difficult time. My whole world fell apart after psychosis and treatment in a psychiatric ward. Nothing was ever the same again after such a profound insult to my being. My aunt's house was a safe place where I was given support but also lots of space. I desperately needed both.

My Background—and My Present Journey

During my childhood my whole family was tyrannized by my father. He was emotionally, physically and sexually abusive. I seem to have become what is sometimes called the "identified patient" in a sick family unit. Aside from me, everyone else in my family thrived after they left our family home. My mother left my father when I was seventeen and remarried a good man. My sister became a surgeon. My brother became a very successful MBA in finance. My other brother, with a heart more like mine, became extremely successful in the non-profit sector. Yet even I, on so many psychiatric drugs, did have a career for a good twelve years as a social worker in HIV and then in mental health—until the drugs completely disabled me.

I think the reason the rest of my family thrived more than I did is that everyone's pain but mine was buried. It seems perhaps that that is still the case.

As I come off the psychiatric drugs the pain that the drugs were helping me hide from is now coming forth. This is my newfound journey. I wasn't ready to start this journey until I moved three thousand miles away from my family—and now I am once again reclaiming my mind, my emotions and my soul. I do not see that in my two surviving siblings. (My older brother, with whom I was close, died a year and a half ago, of cancer.) My remaining siblings and I have no relationship whatsoever because what is of value to them means nothing to me. They value the status and the material rewards of their careers. I instead look to the world and want to change it. I am an activist. I had to get away from my family to find the source of my present pain and to have the courage to stop the drugs and find myself. I am not recovered yet, because I fell into the trap of psychiatry's lies. But I am in tune with what feels like my purpose as I do my work and my research—and I live my life.

I am still healing and my relationships with my family are mostly distant. It needs to be this way, I think. They cannot begin to appreciate the journey I am treading and do not know how to support me. It is not that they don't love me in their own way, because they do, but their energy is not helpful at this juncture and would instead be harmful to me. Instead my "adopted" family consists of my husband, who has been a wonderful, loving and necessary support, other psychiatric survivors in the movement, and numerous friends I've made throughout my life who accept me for who I am. I also have two cats and a dog who are in my extended family. My oldest cat has been with me nineteen years. One bonds with these critters in ways that to this day surprise me.

My mother is a kind woman who has always loved me and supported me to the best of her ability. I love her and she has helped me financially when I've sought expensive alternative care in recent years. That said, we are not similar and do not understand one another emotionally or intellectually. But she accepts me as I am completely. I will forever be grateful for that, though I mourn our inability to be close. Still, some day I hope to bridge the gap.

My closest brother, who died a year and a half ago, understood my spirit. He comes to me in my dreams. I love him and he is still with me.

Two years ago I stopped calling my father. At that time I spent a week helping him move to the town where my sister lives because he had become too old to live far from care. For over twenty years I had never spent time alone with him because the last time I did so, when I was about twenty-one, he made a sexual pass at me.

My experience with him two years ago was awful. He yelled at me, completely losing it, for putting a broken toenail in the bathroom garbage can. He found that disgusting. Since I was in the process of withdrawing from psychiatric drugs and emotionally vulnerable I was not able to process that well, especially in light of his history of abusing me. I have now stopped interacting with him. The toenail verbal abuse was just the most ludicrous of his abuses on that trip.

When I went back home, three thousand miles away, I stopped what had been weekly calls to check in on him. I decided I didn't want his energy in my life anymore. I wanted to heal without his influence. And he has not once tried to call me and see how I am doing. It's been a bit over two years.

I am not happy with the state of my family relations. I am Italian and have very strong Italian values about what family should be. I wish, for example, that I had relationships with my nieces and nephews. I crave these relationships. My family is not what I would like it to be. I have fought for decades to make it happen and am still learning to let go of that dream. I suspect I will never be best friends with my big sister. My little brother thinks I'm really weird and I suspect that we too will never be close. And the only brother who understood me is dead.

My mom remains. I have hope for our future. She has indeed, regardless of imperfection, loved me unconditionally all these years, and perhaps that love is what has allowed me to find myself all these years later—that love and the distance between me and everyone else.

Chapter 23

Best Friends with Mom

by Daniel Mackler

> Editors' Introduction: *Daniel Mackler (co-author of this volume), a graduate of Swarthmore College, is a psychotherapist, filmmaker and writer in New York City. The founder of the website www.iraresoul.com, Daniel is also the director of the documentary film* Take These Broken Wings, *on recovery from schizophrenia without medication (starring Joanne Greenberg) and the co-editor (with David Garfield, M.D.) of* Beyond Medication: Therapeutic Engagement and the Recovery From Psychosis. *Prior to his work as a therapist he performed as a musician for children—in schools, libraries, birthday parties, and on the radio. After college he had a semi-breakdown and lived with his mother for two years.*

Aside from one episode of being sent to a therapist as a young teenager for fighting in school, I never had any involvement with the mental health system until I was in my twenties. I had finished university, and had done well there, earning a degree in biology, but had been clueless about what I wanted to do with my life. So I traveled, for about a year and a half, around Europe, Asia, and the United States—doing occasional menial work to finance the next leg of travel. But I became very depressed as my travels wore on, mostly because I wasn't finding what I was looking for: close friends, a girlfriend, any sort of career, or anything to really keep me grounded in one place. So at the age of twenty-four I ended up living with my mother, sleeping on her small apartment's living room couch in New York City. I felt like I had failed, and by societal standards—and the standards of my dreams—I had.

Meanwhile, I had a lot of ideas that others labeled as grandiose: that I was no longer meant to do "average" work, that I should be recognized for my "specialness" and picked out of the "masses" for some great, non-entry level job, and that employers should just hire me for my "specialness" immediately, without even a résumé or decent work history. This, of course, was unrealistic, as most everyone told me. (And my eighty-five year old grandmother, lacking self-control, went so far as to voice what everyone was thinking and called me "delusional"). But since I had my mother's apartment to live in, and my mother told me I could live there as long as I liked or needed, I wasn't under much external pressure to "face reality." Also, my mom paid for my food and didn't charge me any rent, and the little money I had left over from traveling allowed me to get around town and occasionally socialize with friends.

But my depression worsened. I felt like a nobody, a nothing, and my sense of alienation from society and from my peers, who were all working and struggling to build "realistic" careers, increased. They didn't relate well to me, and I didn't relate well to them. I was sad and lonely and spent a lot of my free time hanging out with my mother and discussing my problems deeply with her. She was recently divorced from my father and was lonely herself, so we made a good pair, though in hindsight it was clearly emotionally incestuous. She was my best friend.

I'd always been very close with her as a kid. She paid a lot of special attention to me, for better and for worse, and I was desperate for her love and approval, which she often gave. I have later found out that other relatives felt we were "over-bonded," and I have since seen that my childhood history involved me meeting a lot of her love needs that my father wasn't meeting. This gave me a sense of value in my life—though it definitely contributed to many of my later emotional conflicts.

After a few months living with her, I sank into deeper misery. I started getting a terrifying feeling that I was never going to climb out of the pit of living on her couch and feeling like a societal loser. It was a horrible feeling, and yet I still couldn't bring myself to find realistic work. I tried to get fancy jobs and never even got called back—and I blamed *them* for it. They couldn't see how special I was! (It couldn't have helped that I grew a ponytail and a beard, and resisted even wearing a tie to their corporate interviews.)

Then I found my salvation—writing. I had always loved reading, and I had always wanted to write a book, so I embarked on a journey to become the next great American novelist. I devoted hours and hours each day, seven days a week, to crafting a book about my life and travels—working diligently at the computer in my mother's bedroom while she was off at work. I slept only a few hours a night and was up at work as soon as she closed the apartment door behind her—and I worked until the minute she returned home ten hours later. I lived with what now were truly grandiose fantasies of fame, massive societal acceptance, and adoring crowds. I even dreamed about it at night. I felt like this success was inevitable—right there at the fingertips of my imagination.

Needless to say, it didn't happen—though I did finish the book after about four months. But almost no one was interested. My family—my mother and sister—read it, and thought it was fairly good, but their tone of voice told me they didn't feel it was conventionally marketable. I got a literary agent for a short time, but he soon dropped me with no explanation—and I never found anyone else in the field who was even a quarter of the way interested. Mostly when I tried to market it, people treated me like I was odd or worse…especially after they found out I was unemployed and living with my mother.

I crashed. I felt rotten. I felt ashamed of myself, and didn't want to tell people about my life situation. I even sometimes told lies about where I was living—or pretended that I was just temporarily living with my mother and would soon be traveling again. Meanwhile, I considered becoming "homeless by choice" and just disappearing into nothingness—wandering the streets with no money and even becoming a street preacher. I even considered suicide—thankfully *very* briefly. At that point I took my mother's suggestion and went to the local Medicaid office to see about getting on free state health insurance—so I could go to free therapy (also her suggestion)—but I just couldn't follow through. The whole process felt too humiliating. Plus, I couldn't bear the possibility that they might tell me something was really psychologically wrong with me.

(In later years I learned that my family bandied around the term "bipolar" for me, and "mentally ill" as well, especially once I started getting in touch with my anger. I was extremely offended by this label and hated the feeling of being pathologized. It cut me to the core. Some people in my family even wanted me to go to a psychiatrist for a medication evaluation—for a mood stabilizer, or maybe even an antipsychotic. That sickened me. I felt like they had stuck a big black spot on my forehead. The only time in my life I had ever taken anything resembling a psychiatric medication was Benadryl for insomnia, which my mother gave me out of her own prescription when I was a teenager. At first I liked that it helped me sleep, but I soon came to hate the medication, because I became psychologically dependent on it—and terrified to try to sleep without it. I eventually refused to take it anymore, and found other non-drug ways to get to sleep.)

Meanwhile, living with my mother, I felt like I had become a child again, with "adults" trying to control my actions and make the important decisions about my life. This kicked up a feeling of desperation in me. Over the next year I struggled to find fancy work (complete failure), spent another four months writing a new book (which almost no one read), worked as a low-pay camp counselor for a summer (interesting, but a humiliating occupation for a college-educated twenty-five year old), tried to lean on my now cold college degree (failed again), considered applying to graduate school (but had no idea what to study), and then even wrote a third book (which only one person read, and didn't much like). I was swinging back and forth, a few months at a time, between hopelessness and hope, self-hatred and "grandiose" self-love, misery and excitement.

All the while my mother and I remained the best of friends—and had deep and passionate talks almost every night. She basically acted as my therapist, and I leaned on her emotionally, financially, and socially. The only thing she did that really infuriated me, though, was suggesting I go to therapy. I adamantly refused. No way! No stranger was going to pick apart my brain and tell me I had problems! (I probably would have been labeled with Major Depression, or maybe Bipolar.)

During this time my friends, building fledgling careers, mostly pulled away from me, which caused me to lean on my mother even more. At this time my sister, a year and a half younger than I, came to stay with us for a couple of months, and we fought constantly. She criticized my lifestyle and felt I had been "going off the deep end" and was "living in la-la land." That hurt, especially because it rang so true somewhere inside me. I hated her then, and wasn't so nice in return, which didn't help, because she wasn't in the greatest place in her life either, having problems of her own. We even came to blows once—slapping mostly—and I ended up spitting in her face once after she punched me and knocked off my glasses. It was totally awful. It was like the worst of my teenage years coming back to haunt me in my mid-twenties. I felt like a maniac. And the worst thing was that I had no one safe with whom I could talk about it.

Finally my sister moved out and got her own apartment (after getting a fancy job), and my attitude toward her was "good riddance." I hated anything and anyone that challenged my hermetically sealed bubble of denial. And frankly, I now see that my mom was nurturing that bubble, even though she wasn't aware of it. She thought all her support was helping me.

Then came the shift—painful at first, but ultimately the path to my liberation: my mother found a boyfriend, and they fell in love. I was terrified of what it meant for me, poor little hopeless dependent me, and I was envious of him. And in fairness, he didn't like me much either—probably seeing me "realistically" in some ways, though he could be cruel in other ways, including offering blunt, unsolicited "reality checks" that kiboshed our conversations.

After a few months my mother decided to move in with him, and she broke the news to me: she was giving up our (that is, her) apartment. And since I couldn't afford it (or even one-tenth of it) I had to move out, because she said I couldn't move in with her and her boyfriend. And I was so depressed and lost that I actually *would have* considered moving in with her and her boyfriend had she offered it.

I panicked. I thought more about becoming homeless. I even called my dad, with whom I was distant, and asked him for a loan of a few thousand dollars. I didn't even know what I would do with the money—perhaps travel again. My mother then intervened and told me *not* to take money from my father. (Good call!) Her new boyfriend was advising her that I needed to "pony up" and get a job, any job, and just start working. In my desperation I now even considered trying to get on Medicaid and disability, because I felt disabled, but I couldn't bring myself to go that route. I hated "the system" too much—and the idea of leaning on it for help was too humiliating.

So I started going to temp agencies, which was a real step down from my fantasies of fame and salvation. But a step down or not, none would hire me, because I'd never worked an office job—and frankly, I also looked quite scruffy, with very long hair and a beard that I resented trimming. Not administrative assistant material. I talked it over with my mother and she suggested I clean up my act, shave and cut my hair (I did the former, ignored the latter), and buy a secondhand suit and tie. (I spent my last money on that, as I was near broke.)

My sister's boyfriend then helped me update my résumé, and he helped me make it more palatable by suggesting I fill in the time gaps with jobs that I hadn't really done—but could pretend I'd done if need be. (I hated lying, but I was desperate.) It helped. One agency, liking that I could type so fast—thank God for all that book-writing!—gave me a weeklong assignment as a secretary at a software development firm, and I began work.

That was one of the greatest weeks of my life. My self-esteem shot up instantly, and to my surprise, my attitude started to shift. The worst of my depression went away immediately, and yet I didn't feel "manic" at all. I hadn't felt so good in over two years—since I'd arrived at my mother's. I started taking better care of myself, including eating better, shopping with my own money, jogging in nearby Central Park, and practicing better hygiene—like shaving every day (hadn't done that in years), showering daily (not in years as well), brushing my teeth after breakfast (as opposed to after lunch… or later), and wearing deodorant (which I'd often gone weeks without, because I felt "special" people were allowed to stink, and the world be damned!).

And I did well at work. The software firm liked me, because I gave them my all, doing anything they asked of me and working all the overtime they wanted. My weeklong assignment extended into two weeks, then three, then a month, which made me feel great. I was ultra-accommodating with them, and felt like a million bucks, so grateful to be a part of a work team, a part of the give and take of the world, and a part of the paycheck-receiving population. I hadn't realized just how demoralizing—and stigmatizing—it had been to be out of that loop.

I saved enough in my final months at my mother's to afford rent on a room-share in another part of New York City, and I moved into someone else's apartment. It surprised me how extremely painful it was to move out of my mom's. Hiding in her bathroom, I cried before I left, and couldn't help but see how incredibly attached I'd become to her, which was embarrassing because I was now three weeks shy of age twenty-six. Sadness or no, I didn't let it stop me from moving out—not that I had any choice. Her lease was up and I was out.

At first I was lonely in my new apartment and new neighborhood, but I felt an odd and deep sense of hope—like this wasn't a "delusional" path anymore, and really had potential to grow. And it did grow, though it took a while. I still hung out with my mother a fair amount, and would go over to her new apartment and have dinner from time to time with her and her boyfriend. We no longer spent hours discussing our intimate lives like co-therapists, and the better boundaries actually helped us get along better. In the past we had bickered like a long-married couple; now we were more respectful. I have to admit, though, that for a while I resented her for kicking me out and just throwing me over for the new guy.

But actually it saved my life. I'm terrified to think what would have happened to me had she not found that boyfriend and given up her apartment. For whatever reason, I lacked the power to get out on my own. I was truly stuck in psychological molasses. I think I might have stayed there forever—and perhaps eventually really gotten on medication, gone on disability, or maybe even gone in a worse direction. I felt like I had been granted a reprieve on life. My friends returned to my life, and I made new ones, and after a year I got better and more interesting jobs at different companies, and actually started earning more money and more respect from my coworkers. In time I even started meeting women—women my age—who liked me.

It's now been ten years since I moved out of my mother's apartment. She and I have had some rough years in there—years in which I went to therapy willingly, paid my own way, and didn't garner psychiatric diagnoses that made me feel like a pathological object, years in which I actually was able to explore my childhood, and also explore those two years of sinking into self-hating hell on her couch. I went through periods of resentment at her, and at my father too, and some of these years were ugly and painful, with fights and recriminations. But that has mostly passed. I now spend time with my parents once again—and my sister too—not a lot, but some. And now we have a much higher degree of mutual respect. I pay my bills, and I have my own apartment, my own group of close friends, and my own personal interests. And I have a career I love and respect. I'm a psychotherapist now—ironically enough—and I struggle to be the kind of therapist I would have wanted back when I was in my mid-twenties—the kind of therapist I strongly sensed I would have been unlikely to find. Meanwhile, as a consumer, I no longer have any involvement with the mental health field, though for a few years I did go to Al-Anon, the support group for friends and family members of alcoholics (as alcoholism does run in my family).

I don't regret what I went through, because it totally helped me gain perspective on my life and the lives of others, and helped me realize some of my vulnerabilities and susceptibilities. And it has made me more humble. In the past I would have been much more likely to judge someone who went through what I went through, and actually that is why I was so judgmental of myself when I went through it. I didn't know how to be compassionate with myself—or take care of myself properly. Now I see things—or hope I do—in more perspective. My parents loved me in some ways, but they also made mistakes in their attitudes and behavior. They were trying to help me, but it wasn't always the help I really needed, or even thought I needed. Thankfully I came out the other side.

Chapter 24

Listening to Each Other: My Mother and I

by Janet Foner

> Editors' Introduction: *Janet Foner, a psychiatric survivor and advocate based in Pennsylvania, was hospitalized in her twenties and placed on antipsychotic drugs. Fully recovered, Janet holds a master's degree in community psychology. She is also a leader in the organization known as Re-evaluation Counseling (RC). RC, also called Co-Counseling, is both a process for emotional healing, and a worldwide network of people who support each other emotionally and promote social justice. She leads Mental Health Liberation workshops in many parts of the United States and other countries. Janet is a wife and a mother of two young adults. In her spare time, she designs and makes quilts, cooks, and redecorates various rooms in her house.*

In the Hospital

It was 1967, I was twenty-one years old, and about to graduate from college. I was on a locked ward of a mental hospital in Pittsburgh, Pennsylvania, where I would stay for ten months. I do not know what my diagnosis was, but from what my psychiatrist told me, and from the fact that I was given Thorazine and Stelazine, I guess that it was schizophrenia. There had been no commitment procedure at first. I was later tricked into a "voluntary" commitment, as I did not know my rights at the time. I certainly hadn't volunteered to go in the hospital.[42]

A few days after being admitted, I complained to my psychiatrist about the feeling that I couldn't sit still (akathisia), and he stopped the Stelazine, but he kept me on a huge amount of Thorazine. The first time I had Thorazine, the dose was so high that I passed out. It made me feel extremely tired, ready for bed before 8:00 p.m., and more depressed than I had been. It also affected my vision negatively, made me temporarily forget how to draw (I'm an artist, so that was scary), gave me hallucinations (I'd never had them before the drug—or after I stopped it), and caused me to gain thirty pounds, among other things.

After being put in seclusion twice for trying to refuse drugs, I finally accepted the idea that I "needed" the Thorazine, and took it voluntarily, and continued to do so for about seven months after I got out of the hospital. While in the hospital, I had psychotherapy for an hour four times a week, and later twice a week as an outpatient, for a total of two years and four months. The therapy was fairly helpful, in that my psychiatrist listened well, but I didn't find the analysis or advice useful. I also found the experience of living in a mental hospital extremely depressing and hard.

How I Ended Up in the Hospital

I was born into a family in crisis in September, 1945, right after World War II, the Holocaust, and the bomb being dropped on Hiroshima. My parents, born in the United States, were children of Eastern European Jewish immigrants. While I was in the womb, my dad almost died. My mother was a month pregnant with me when my dad, an army captain, got sick with what they thought was a rare form of polio. She (and I, in the womb) spent six months at the hospital with him helping to save his life. By the time I was born, his illness had ended, and he was in a rehabilitation hospital, permanently paralyzed from the waist down. He didn't come home for another two years. I believe I was born feeling terrified, sad, and

---

[42] Janet Foner's note to the reader: I don't believe that so-called "mental illnesses" exist, but that discussion is not included here due to space limitations. For my view on that subject, please see my chapter, "Surviving the 'Mental Health' System with Co-Counseling," pp.107-124, in the book, *Psychosocial Approaches to Deeply Disturbed Persons*. Peter R. Breggin and E. Mark Stern (Eds.). New York: Haworth Press, 1996.

needing a dad, and I look that way in my baby pictures. At any rate, I only rarely felt upbeat or hopeful as a child.

By the time I was in high school, I did not "fit in" for many reasons. I was very unpopular and believed that there was something wrong with me. My sister and I were close in early childhood, but didn't get along very well after that. She was three and a half years older than I and had never really recovered from the events surrounding my father's illness. She was rebellious, ran away from home at age six, and was seen as the "problem child" in our large, extended family. I stayed quiet and in the background to avoid seeming like her.

My mother, who had far more on her plate than anyone should have had to handle, yelled and screamed a lot, mostly at my sister. Frequently our home was like a "mine field," and I never knew what would erupt next. However, my mother was also often extremely warm and loving. She was wise, principled, a great listener, and often had lots of attention for young people—and she was a persistent advocate for my dad. Many people wished she was their mother. Throughout my childhood she listened to me and held me close in her arms as she comforted me about whatever problem I had. I was extremely close to her.

My father and I were never close. Feeling both ashamed of his disability and inadequate as a father due to that, he could not relate well to me, emotionally speaking. Although he was also somewhat strict, he was a fine, friendly, honest, courageous man who, in spite of the hardships of his disability, never gave up on having a good life.

At seventeen, I had a very close boyfriend whom I hoped to marry. We dated for four years, but he broke up with me just before my senior year of college. I was heartbroken—and also scared about the future, because as a painting major, it was unlikely that I would find a job after college. That spring, I became overwhelmed with feelings when three tall, dark, and handsome guys all asked me for dates in the same week. I started crying and trembling a lot, as well as feeling on top of the world. I also began writing and talking in metaphors, I think because things were happening too fast for me to assess logically. But I wasn't worried, because I had never been told to hold in my emotions.

My mother, however, became terrified. Her father had died in a mental hospital after being there for three years. On the advice of our family doctor she took me to Western Psychiatric Institute. I did not want to go, and was angry about her taking me there. I didn't know that being angry in the admissions office of a hospital would get me locked up. But that's what happened.

My family, including most of my large extended family, was pretty helpful during and after my hospitalization. My mother came to see me at every allowable visiting time. During my first few days there I wanted desperately to go home. I was terrified from being on a locked ward, from having been locked in seclusion—a small padlocked room with nothing but a mattress—and from the effects of the drugs.

One day early in my stay I remember walking down the hall with a nurse and my mother. I said I felt like I was going to vomit. The nurse insisted, in a very mean tone, that I wasn't going to. My mother and I went in my room, at which point I vomited. She cleaned me up, held me close, and listened to me cry, comforting and calming me. She brought flowers most times she came, and stayed with me even after we had an argument one time.

Until I was allowed home on weekends, my dad came to see me after work every week, even though visiting any kind of hospital was emotionally difficult for him. I remember once I was crying, with both of my parents there, about being stuck in the hospital and feeling like I would never get out. My dad said, "Just take it one day at a time, and you'll get out of here." That meant a lot to me, especially since I knew he knew what he was talking about.

After I'd been in the hospital for nine months, my parents planned a vacation to Puerto Rico—but they didn't want to leave me in the hospital while they were gone. My psychiatrist allowed me to go to Puerto Rico with them, with the agreement that I would come back to the hospital for another month after I returned—to make sure I was ready for discharge.

When I left for Puerto Rico, I had been in the hospital for so long that I was afraid I wasn't okay enough to "make it" on the outside. What I discovered instead was that it wasn't any harder outside the hospital than in. If more mental patients had parents who supported them emotionally as well as mine did, I'm sure there would be fewer patients left in the mental health system.

Out of the Hospital

After I got out of the hospital, my parents did some kind things which helped me greatly. For instance, just after I was released and had moved back home, they were going out to dinner and wanted me to join them. I didn't feel like I could go because I thought people in the restaurant would know I had been a mental patient and would talk about me. My mother insisted that I go, and this was one of the best things she did for me. I needed to re-enter society, not isolate myself, and somehow she knew that. When I went out to dinner that night, I realized that no one noticed me—and that my fears were obviously unfounded.

After I got out of the hospital, though, my mother was sometimes a hard person to be around. For instance, although I was in no condition to look for work, she was determined that I get a job, and she pressured me a lot. I was kind of "out of it," still on psychiatric drugs, and overwhelmed with difficult feelings from the long hospitalization. I was very depressed, felt ashamed, had no self-confidence, and felt "weird." On top of that, I had no idea what I wanted to do—or possibly could do—with my life, let alone what job I might be interested in.

But to keep my mom from getting too angry with me, I called various places to try to find a job. While this was hard on me in a certain way, it was also helpful, because no one else aside from her assumed I would or could do anything with my life. Her insistence finally pushed me to get a job as a substitute art teacher in the public school system. It was a perfect job for me in that it was easy to get, it was work for which no one had high expectations, and I didn't need confidence in order to do it. Also, it allowed me to work part-time, so I could gradually ease into the job world. Best of all, it allowed me to leave home and get an apartment—with another ex-psychiatric inmate I knew from the hospital. This let me have more "breathing space" away from my family, and I had very little trouble getting along with them after that. And despite my mother's insistence that I get a job, my parents subsidized my rent when I didn't have enough work as a substitute teacher. I appreciated this greatly.

Around that same time, I got off of psychiatric drugs. My psychiatrist, who knew I didn't want the drugs, had been gradually reducing the amount I was taking all along. Once I stopped taking the drugs, I felt *much* better! I was able to think clearly and stay awake at last! My life got better quickly after that. The next summer, I married one of the three guys mentioned earlier, and moved out of state to the town where he was working—where no one knew me, or knew I had been a mental patient. I only saw my psychiatrist once more after that, and since then I have never again been on psychiatric drugs or in the mental health system as a patient or client.

All of this was exactly what I needed to do for my recovery—to get away from the situations, people, and places that caused my original difficulties, and from the mental health system that had greatly exacerbated these difficulties. I learned from my experiences in the mental health system that I was a lot stronger than I had thought, that I could survive extreme emotional pain and come out on top of it, that nothing could get me down, and that I could rely on friends and family to be there for me when times were tough. I had also learned to grab onto the positive in my life and go with it, to keep moving forward, and not let negative feelings stop me.

Yet I still had a lot of healing work to do, particularly in relation to my mother. About five years after I was in the hospital, I accidentally came into contact with Re-evaluation Counseling, also known as both RC and Co-Counseling. I loved how well the process works. Co-Counseling allowed me to understand both what happened to me emotionally in relation to my hospital experience and how to help my mother understand what had happened to me.

RC also helped me figure out how to move against the oppression I had faced while in the mental health system—and how to change things in the larger society vis-à-vis that oppression. In 1978, about five years after I started doing Co-Counseling, I began to work with others to build a network of psychiatric survivors and ex-therapy clients within RC, and am still doing that. In 1992, I became the International Liberation Reference Person for Mental Health Liberation within RC.

My mother was puzzled about why I was doing this work. She thought I had been helped by my stay in the hospital and didn't understand why I wanted to change the mental health system. I explained to her that although my psychiatrist and some of the other staff were somewhat helpful to me, the net effect of being in the hospital was very hard on me. I told her that being forced to be in seclusion—for eight hours when admitted to the hospital, and for four hours a few days later—were extremely damaging experiences. (I am still recovering emotionally from them.) She was shocked to find out that I had been in seclusion. I had thought that the hospital had told my family what they were doing, but they hadn't. I now realized that if they had, my mother probably would have tried to get me released immediately. I also realized that the silence and mystery surrounding mental health treatments must be interrupted,

Listening to Each Other: My Mother and I 149

so that patients and family members can understand each other better. From this conversation, my mother began to grasp what I was trying to do in my life.

Over many years, my mother kept trying to understand more about what had happened to me. This was probably partly because she felt bad that she had been the one who took me to the mental hospital. We had many conversations, usually frustrating for me, because she didn't understand my perspective: that there had been nothing essentially wrong with me when I entered the mental hospital. Certainly, I didn't need hospitalization.

My mother knew that I did Co-Counseling, and thought of it as therapy for me. She didn't understand that it isn't therapy. It is done as an equal exchange of attention between two peers, each taking a separate turn to be listened to and thought about by the other. I finally decided to teach my mother RC to try to help her understand me better, as well as to help her with her own issues. At the end of the first class I held, with her and a few close friends of ours, she realized that this was not therapy at all. She said, "This is like what we always do!" I agreed.

For the next twelve years, until she died in 2004, each time I visited her (about two or three times a year), I continued to teach her RC. Somewhere around 2002, she and I had an amazing phone conversation. For some reason she brought up my mental hospital experience again. I said (which I'd said many times before) that I hadn't needed to be hospitalized. All I had needed was a few good Co-Counseling sessions and I would have been fine. She said, "But you weren't in good enough shape to be in RC then."

(To be accepted into a formal RC class, one has to have good enough attention to be able to listen well to others.)

I replied that I had been.

She said, "You weren't sleeping or eating!"

I replied, "I missed one night of sleep and one breakfast! I just needed someone to listen to me."

She then asked, "You mean I should have just taken you home and held you while you cried?"

"Yes!"

She said, "I am so sorry that I was misinformed by the doctors!"

For me, that was a breakthrough conversation. My mother finally had understood things from my point of view. We regained a lot of closeness that day.

Chapter 25

What They Don't Tell You, You Can Tell Your Family

by Oryx Cohen

> Editors' Introduction: *Oryx Cohen, M.P.A., co-founder of Freedom Center, is a leader in the international consumer/survivor/ex-patient (c/s/x) movement and has helped to spearhead an innovative peer-run approach to recovery, healing, and community. Oryx serves on several international and national boards and committees, including the International Network Toward Alternatives for Recovery (INTAR). Currently he is the Co-Director of the Western Massachusetts Recovery Learning Community, and is an adjunct faculty member of the psychology department at Westfield State College in Massachusetts. Oryx was diagnosed with bipolar disorder and placed on antipsychotics and mood stabilizers, but has safely withdrawn and is fully recovered. He is married, has a young child, and has another on the way.*

How I Landed in the Psychiatric System

After moving across the country to Massachusetts for graduate school in 1999, I had a very interesting, strange, wonderful, spiritual, and terrible experience that landed me in the psychiatric ward. During the first stressful weeks of class I lost touch with physical reality and convinced myself I could fly my car, which led to an almost-fatal car accident. Luckily I was the only one hurt. I was airlifted by helicopter to Worcester Memorial Hospital in Worcester, Massachusetts. After a few short days in the trauma unit I was transferred—broken collarbone, head wound, and all—to the locked inpatient psychiatric ward on the eighth floor. I was twenty-six years old.

The psychiatrist there diagnosed me with bipolar disorder and told me I would have to be on psychiatric medications for the rest of my life. I had been raised in a hippie family who believed in natural remedies, and I was terrified of the drugs. It became clear, though, that they would not let me leave the hospital—which I desperately wanted to do—unless I took the Risperdal and Depakote they prescribed. So I took the medications—extremely high doses of both—and they released me from the hospital after eight days.

Within two months I was sleeping sixteen hours a day and had gained twenty pounds. I had trouble concentrating, my hands trembled uncontrollably, and I vomited from nausea a few times per week. I soon found out that these were all "side effects" of the medication. I was well on my way to becoming a career mental patient.

My Family and My Background

Despite my parents divorcing when I was five years old, which was difficult for me, I remember being very happy as a child. I was always athletic, I loved sports, and I did quite well in school. I was also extremely sensitive. When I encountered verbally abusive basketball coaches in high school, it severely affected my confidence and happiness, resulting in many years of difficult struggle that culminated in the car crash.

When I was growing up, my mom and dad lived a couple of blocks apart in Eugene, Oregon. My younger brother and I saw them both regularly. We lived primarily with our dad, but we also had a bed at our mom's too. My brother and I were always very close *and* very competitive, which was a double-edged sword. We pretty much did everything together and shared many of the same friends. There was quite a bit of tension between us, though, because of the divorce and the fact that my brother had lived in New Mexico with our mom for over a year. I always had the role of the "good" child and my brother that of the "rebel"—picking fights with our parents and finding creative ways to get attention. Overall my family all loved each other and enjoyed each other's company (even our divorced parents were cordial), but we definitely had our moments of chasing each other around the house, loud arguments, and angry outbursts.

Both my parents lived in Oregon at the time of the car accident. My near-death experience shook their world apart and they flew to Massachusetts to be with me for several weeks. Actually, though, I had more face-to-face interactions with my brother and grandfather then, because they lived nearby—and because I lived with my grandpa for about four months, in Rhode Island, after the hospitalization.

When I was first diagnosed, my family relied on the counsel of the doctors and mental health professionals. They needed somewhere to turn, they needed some answers, and they had always been taught to trust the medical establishment. I remember while I was in the hospital—and in the months after being released—having heated arguments with my family about the legitimacy of my diagnosis and about my desire to live without medications. I believe that they cared for me and wanted to do their best, but they now saw me as broken, as having this lifelong illness. I rejected then and still reject the very idea of "mental illness." I would get very emotional when telling them that I was not "sick" or "diseased," yet my intensity only served to confirm their worst fears.

To make matters worse, I had checked myself into the psychiatric ward "voluntarily"—and became very upset when the staff did not allow me to leave immediately. All I wanted was to go to my grandfather's where I could try to recover from this serious trauma. I accepted that I had lost touch with reality—and I only wanted to pull my life back together in a loving, peaceful environment. Tying shoelaces together and "learning" how to go grocery shopping as a part of occupational therapy just wasn't doing it for me.

What Worked For Me...And What Didn't

Looking back, I realize that my strong emotions—as legitimate as they were—certainly did not help my situation. For instance, when I was in the hospital I had several intense arguments with my mom. I thought that because she'd basically been a hippie her whole life she would see my side of things, but instead she sided with the doctors. I remember one meeting where my treatment team was telling me (in front of my family) that I was mentally ill and would have to be on medications for the rest of my life. I vehemently disagreed and stormed out of the meeting, slamming the door behind me. My mom followed me to my room and we proceeded to have a very loud argument. Outbursts like these probably cost me a few more days on the ward. I think I would have been there even longer than eight days had my brother not called them regularly demanding that they let me go—*and* had I not *had* somewhere to go. His advocacy and my grandfather's willingness to take me in were crucial.

Staying at my grandfather's house was a rollercoaster experience as I learned how to deal most effectively with my family. It took me a while to learn that my strong emotions were not helping. Instead I came to discover that my academic and mostly Jewish family responded best to logic, reason, and research. After my hospitalization they bought several mainstream books about what bipolar disorder is and how to "treat" it. Of course these books were written by conventional psychiatrists and were strongly oriented toward the medical model.

Something told me that these books did not have all the answers and that the best way to convince my family of a different path was to do my own research. I was very lucky in that the graduate program I was in at the University of Massachusetts allowed me to do an independent study that semester on bipolar disorder, the mental health system, and the resulting public policy implications. So while I was recovering from my broken collarbone, head trauma, and altered experience I embarked on this life-changing project.

My grandfather's quiet and even sterile house and neighborhood proved to be the perfect environment for me to concentrate on research—and recover from my episode of mania. I quickly found that all the medical research pretty much said the same things about the theorized causes and treatments of bipolar disorder, but what was so interesting to me was that they discussed only that: *theories*. Every article ended by saying that there was not enough evidence to suggest organic brain disease, that there are no testable biological markers, etc. I was surprised to see that even the medical journal articles seemed to disprove the chemical imbalance theory. It was obvious that my Depakote for "bipolar" was not at all like insulin for diabetes, as my psychiatrists all parroted to me.

What was even more interesting, however, was the amount of research I found *supporting* other theories, such as empowerment models and trauma models. Everywhere I turned I found that people were recovering from these types of severe diagnoses—even schizophrenia—and most were doing it without medication! I discovered the long-term research studies on Loren Mosher's Soteria House and the work of Courtney Harding. I found out about the

National Empowerment Center in Massachusetts and MindFreedom International in Oregon. Here was an entire community and movement of people who totally affirmed what I believed in my heart to be true. Finding people like Laurie Ahern and David Oaks gave me strength and inspiration to press forward—and fight for my life.

Armed with this research, my strong emotions waning a bit, I was now ready to approach my family. I knew, even if subconsciously, that I could never be successful in going off of my medications if I did not have the support of those closest to me.

My family is very intelligent, and the evidence I presented to them was quite logical and compelling—and they responded well to it. My mother, father, and brother were particularly supportive because I think they had already begun to question the overmedicalization of society in general. My grandfather was a more difficult sell as he had been raised in a generation that revered doctors not only as MDs but almost as "M-Deities." But my grandfather is also a really kind and generous man, so he did ultimately support me on what I wanted to try.

At this point I tapered off my medication, and for a time it worked. However, after almost two years of solid recovery, in which I lived medication-free, I did have another altered experience and subsequent hospitalization. This was in 2002, after my graduation. Despite this new mania being an extremely intense and difficult time for me, my family had already seen me succeed a different way, and they continued to support me in trying to heal holistically. Family at that time included my girlfriend, whom I'd met in graduate school.

My girlfriend, with no prior training or experience with these situations, did all the right things during my "psychosis." First of all, she stayed with me, and was completely present with me the entire time. She knew I feared going back to the hospital almost as much as death, so she didn't make that call until I was so worn out with the experience that in a moment of clarity I gave her permission. For that reason I did not feel violated. Also, she printed out my "bio" that was posted on the MindFreedom website and took it to the hospital so that the hospital staff would understand that I did not want to take medications. Because of her, my second hospitalization was a much better experience than the first, and I was treated much better the second time around.

After I got out of the hospital, I was completely raw and it took months for me to recover. For the first time in my life I started to have terrifying, heart-pounding, earth-shattering panic attacks. The worst attack came when I went to visit my psychiatrist again. The shame I felt was devastating. This wasn't supposed to happen again. Not to me. Not after all I had been through. I was supposed to be recovered. My girlfriend was driving me to the appointment and it was all coming back to me at once. The car crash. My second altered state. It all hit me like a tsunami and I felt my heart would literally explode. Terror invaded every cell. I felt myself being pulled into the other world again.

What my girlfriend did for me was very simple and potentially lifesaving. On that trip to the psychiatrist she used very simple grounding techniques to get me back to the here-and-now. She asked me about my basketball game the other night. She pointed out the color of the trees. She did whatever it took to keep me in the present and to prevent me from completely dissociating again. With her help, I was able to survive that appointment, slowly get back on my feet, and start making a steady recovery.

She and I are now married and have a baby daughter, a dream I could never have imagined possible ten years ago. I am now thirty-five years old and have also been living for over seven years completely medication- and hospitalization-free.

Concluding Words

I know I am very lucky to have a family and now a wife who are open to a different way of looking at things—and who ultimately support me on my journey. If at all possible, I would recommend to people who are going through similar circumstances to try to educate yourselves and your families about all of your options in your recovery process. If your family is not at all open to listening or does not want to support you for whatever reason, then there are people who will. I know several people who have had to find "new" families because their families of origin became more a part of the problem than the solution. The important thing is to find positive people in your life who you can count on, not as caretakers or providers, but as genuine allies and friends. Of course, it can make life much easier when you can find those people in your immediate family, but forming positive connections with family may not be possible and it is important to understand that close friends can be just as supportive and helpful in the healing process.

Index

Adams, Patch, xi, 125-28
Al-Anon, 141
Alcohol abuse, 35, 52, 53-54, 74, 106, 142
Alcoholics Anonymous, 54
Alienation, 4, 5, 10, 11, 16, 20, 26, 55, 84, 136
Anger
 parents' anger, 15, 16, 21, 36, 147, 153
 your anger, 39-42, 43, 44-45, 67, 85, 101, 106, 108, 109, 137, 145-46
Antidepressants. *see* Medications
Antipsychotics. *see* Medications
Anxiety, 10, 15, 25, 58, 60, 98, 101-2, 107

Bipolar disorder, xi, 9n, 25, 26, 27, 74, 81, 82, 100, 129-30, 137, 138, 151-54
Blame, 16, 21, 45, 100, 116, 136
Boundaries, 31-38, 39, 67, 68, 102, 141
Boundaries, list of potential violations, 34-37
Borderline personality disorder, 64
Breggin, Peter, xii, 28n, 144n

Chemical imbalance, 14, 82, 83, 154
Child abuse, 16, 31-32, 35, 36, 43, 45-46, 91
Childhood history, 31, 32n, 35
Cigarettes, 60, 60n, 106
Co-Counseling, 143, 144n, 148-49
Cohen, Oryx, 3n, 11n, 151-56
Confronting parents, 68, 69, 116-17

Delusions, 5, 9, 63, 97, 101, 129, 136, 141, 151
Denial, 22, 120, 139

Dependency on family/system, 49, 86, 94, 138-39
Depression, 5, 21, 25, 40-41, 54, 82, 100, 102, 105, 109, 115, 120, 131, 135-36, 138-40, 144, 147
Diet, 49, 52-53, 55, 82, 87, 116
Disability, 57, 76, 139, 141, 145
Distance from family of origin, xiii, 45-47, 67-69, 87, 93, 110, 124
Drug abuse, 35, 53-54, 55, 84, 129-31
Dundas, Dorothy, 20n, 50n, 105-11

ECT. *See* Electroconvulsive therapy
Electroconvulsive therapy, xi, 27, 74, 77, 92, 105, 107-8, 110, 114
Emotional abuse, 16, 31-32, 43, 108, 132, 136, 152
Empowerment, 3n, 7, 30, 49, 58, 59, 87, 154, 155
Empathy, 10, 25, 46, 64, 101
Exercise, 51, 54-55, 82, 87

Foner, Janet, 143-49
Forced psychiatric drugging, 27, 82, 87, 130
Forgiveness, 43-47
Friendship, 15, 19, 20, 23, 25-26, 34, 36, 50, 55, 58, 74-75, 77, 84, 92, 105-11, 115-16, 120, 123, 126-27, 133, 135-36, 141, 148-49, 152, 155-56

Genetics, as theoretical cause of psychiatric problems, 14, 15, 23, 23n, 79, 82, 116
Greenberg, Joanne, xi, 20-21, 27n, 50n, 119-24, 135
Grief, 37, 39-42, 43, 45-46, 59, 68, 133
Guilt, 16, 64, 95, 102, 116

Hallucinations. *see* Voices, hearing
Hallucinogenic drugs, 54, 129-30
Hall, Will, 3n, 5n, 30n, 113-117
Hearing Voices. *see* Voices, hearing
Hearing Voices Network, 3n
Hebald, Carol, 16n, 89-96
Hope, xii-xiii, 4-6, 21, 23, 39, 41, 42, 69, 107-8, 110, 126, 134, 138, 140, 145
Hornstein, Gail, ix, 35n
Humiliation, 16, 19, 20, 55, 57, 92, 122, 130, 137-39

Independence, gaining, 3, 6, 7, 13, 15, 17, 34, 36, 60, 76, 86-87, 93, 114, 154
I Never Promised You a Rose Garden (Greenberg), xi, 20, 21, 119
Intimacy, 5, 63, 108, 114, 141
Isolation, 5, 10, 11, 49, 51, 55, 81, 121, 125, 130, 147

Kali, Gianna, 129-134

Lifestyle, changing, 29, 49-55, 68, 138
Lobotomy, 27, 108
Loneliness, 12, 47, 99, 108, 122, 126, 136, 140
Loss, 20-22, 39, 40, 42, 68
LSD. *see* Hallucinogenic drugs

Mackler, Daniel, 20n, 21n, 28n, 135-142
Mania, 63, 98, 131, 154-55
Manic-depression. *see* Bipolar Disorder
Marijuana, 53-54, 84
Maturity, 6, 15, 46, 58, 62
Medication, psychiatric
  as symptom suppressants, 27-28, 44, 51
  benefits versus risks, 28, 51-52, 94, 138
  coming off safely, 28-30, 116, 129-134, 147-48, 155
  dangers from stopping abruptly, xii, 29
  family and, 6, 21, 28, 37, 41, 85, 87, 137, 153
  forced psychiatric drugging, 27, 82, 87, 130
  mainstream psychiatry and, 21, 27-28, 64, 76, 82, 92-93, 100, 116, 131, 144-47, 152-53
  personal choice, xii, 28-30, 62, 76, 113, 131
  recovery and, xi-xii, 9n, 20n, 28, 78, 94, 148, 154-56
  side effects, 28, 54, 75, 77, 82, 94, 100, 131 33, 144, 146-47, 152
Meditation, 116
Mental hospitals. *see* Hospitalization
Miller, Alice, 13n, 32n, 46n
MindFreedom International, 3n, 81, 86, 155
Money, 6, 35, 36, 57-60, 76, 79, 93, 133, 136-41
Morrissey, Matthew, 50n, 51, 97-103
Mourning. *see* Grief
Mushrooms, magic. *see* Hallucinogenic drugs

Neuroleptics. *see* Medications
Nutrition. *see* Diet

Oaks, David, 3n, 50n, 54n, 81-88, 109, 155

Patience, 50
Peer support, 3, 23, 34, 50, 84, 87, 141, 149
Peer support groups, 3n, 11, 23, 50, 54, 58, 116, 141, 113, 151
Perceptions, of "reality", 9-12, 84
Physical abuse, 16, 31, 32, 34, 35, 41, 43, 46, 53, 74, 107, 108, 116, 132, 138-39
Psychiatric diagnosis. *see* Diagnosis
Psychiatric medication. *see* Medication
Psychotherapy. *see* Therapy

Rage, 16, 39-41, 43-45, 90, 93, 94, 98, 114
Re-evaluation counseling [RC]. *see* Co-Counseling
Rejection, feelings of, 16, 26
Religion, 37, 54, 57, 125, 129
Responsibility, 4, 6, 15, 16, 17, 39, 41-42, 45, 49, 58, 59, 68, 79, 102
Restraints, experiences of, xi, 108, 130
Rogers, Annie, 73-80
Role models, 5, 27, 42
Roles, in the family, 13-18, 22, 44, 68, 87, 100, 102, 152

Sadness, 39-40, 44, 59, 105, 136, 140, 144
Seclusion rooms, 106, 108, 130, 144, 146, 148
Schizophrenia, xi-xii, 9n, 15, 20, 25-28, 60n, 64, 73-75, 81-82, 89, 92-94, 100, 105, 109, 113-14, 116, 119, 123, 135, 143, 154
Shock therapy. *see* Electroconvulsive Therapy
Self-esteem, 15-17, 19, 20, 22, 39, 60, 102, 106, 125, 127, 140
Self-love, 41-42, 127, 138
Sex/Sexuality, 31, 37, 94
Sexual abuse, 16, 31, 32, 35, 36, 43, 45, 90-91, 94, 104, 114, 132, 134
covert sexual abuse, 32, 35, 36-37, 92
Shame, 19-23, 61, 63, 94, 95, 98, 122, 137, 145, 147, 156
Siblings, 67, 73-80, 83, 97, 101-2, 107, 114-16, 126, 130, 132-34, 90-91, 95, 97, 102, 111, 120-21, 123, 132, 134, 137-41, 145, 152-55
Sleep
as trigger for psychosis, 51, 97-100
oversleeping, 51, 152
part of healthy lifestyle, 50-52, 55, 130
Spirituality, 43, 54, 116, 129-30, 151
Stigma, 4, 6, 9, 16, 19-23, 57, 140

Suicidal feelings/behavior, 25, 74-76, 82, 92-93, 116, 126, 128, 137
Support, xii, 49-50
of family, 3-4, 6, 13, 15, 21, 49-50, 67-68, 77, 82-83, 87, 101, 111, 123, 126, 132, 146, 155-56
of friends, 20, 23, 25, 34, 50, 55, 77, 105-11, 116, 123, 126-27, 133, 135, 141, 148-49, 155-56
of mental health professionals, 3, 6, 23, 26, 50, 58, 61-65, 79, 93, 100-1, 110, 120-23, 141, 144
of peers, 3, 11, 23, 34, 50, 54, 58, 84, 87, 113, 116, 123, 133, 141, 149, 151
Symptoms, 21, 27-28, 44, 78, 119, 122

***T**ake These Broken Wings* (Mackler), 20, 135
Therapy, 3, 6, 23, 26, 46, 50, 58, 61-65, 79, 93, 100-1, 110, 120-23, 141, 144
Trauma
childhood, 35, 43, 45, 59, 74-75, 90-92, 154
from psychiatric system, 44, 46, 82, 105, 130, 153
intergenerational patterns, 46, 114, 116-17
Twelve Step Groups. *see also* Peer support groups, 54, 58, 141

Voices, hearing, 3n, 5, 35, 35n, 73, 76, 91, 115-16, 120

Whitaker, Robert, ix, 12n, 28n
Williams, Robin, xi, 125
Working, 22, 26, 28, 57-60, 78-79, 86-87, 117, 121-22, 132, 135-36, 138-41, 147
World Health Organization Studies, xii, 28
Wounds, emotional, 3, 15, 32n, 40, 43, 45

Yoga, 55, 113

ISPS-US BOOK SERIES

A Way Out of Madness is the first book in the ISPS-US book series.

ISPS-US, the United States Chapter of the International Society for the Psychological Treatments of the Schizophrenias and Other Psychoses, is a nonprofit organization of mental health professionals, consumers, and family members that promotes the humane, comprehensive, and in-depth treatment of psychotic disorders.

Books for the ISPS-US series are peer-reviewed by an editorial committee.

For more information visit **www.isps-us.org** and **www.isps.org**

THE INTERNATIONAL SOCIETY FOR THE PSYCHOLOGICAL
TREATMENTS OF THE SCHIZOPHRENIAS AND OTHER PSYCHOSES
UNITED STATES CHAPTER

Printed in Great Britain
by Amazon